DOG TRAINING TOOLKIT

A PRACTICAL Approach To A Better Dog-Human Relationship

For Dog Lovers Only

Tim Carter

Founder MyGermanShepherd.Org

Edition 4

Disclaimer

Every dog is special, through its unique genetical heritage, living environment, and personal treatment by its owner or handler, as well as prior and current human and animal contacts.

Accordingly, no suggestions given to a dog owner or handler can ever be right for every dog and its owner regardless of the individual circumstances. It is your and your dog's individual circumstances that may or may not make a certain form of training, care, or remedy successful in your case.

You are encouraged to consciously observe your puppy and adult dog in order to recognize any adverse development as soon as possible, and to apply your own common sense to complement the suggestions made in this book, in light of your individual situation.

Neither the publisher nor the author can be held accountable, neither for the favorable implications of applying any suggestion made in this book, nor for the unfavorable implications. It is your dog's individual situation that will determine the success of any and every suggestion made in this book, and your dog's individual situation as well as your opinion will change with time.

DEDICATION

This book is dedicated to all dogs
misunderstood by their owners

Dogs that wish that their owner reads
the right books

Ah well, that's dogs' wishful thinking...

Contents

What's Missing in ALL Dog Training Books

Most dog books that I read are rather scientific (behavior or health related), nonetheless I may have read well over a hundred dog **training** books.

At some point I realized that none of the dog training books offer any systematization of their training approach. All of them give (more or less useful) *individual tips* how we can train our own dog in certain situations or for certain goals (say obedience, dog tricks, guide dog, etc).

However, none of the advice in the books has any identifiable structure that would allow us to remember which individual training tips are helpful in what situation. Rather, the authors seem to have written down their personal experience with using certain techniques on their own dog - or in case of dog trainers, using the techniques on their clients' dogs.

But dogs aren't all the same. This is why the personal experience a dog trainer has made with all his clients' dogs may not relate to your dog. More so: It may not even relate to the *same* dog some time later. Because a dog's environment and treatment changes over time, and so does the dog.

Sure, there are a few books that say, list the core elements of Dog Obedience Training, or the differences between Puppy Training and Adult Dog Training, or how to train aggressive dogs. But honestly, who can remember 200 pages of prose?

I can't! I can read tons of material, but without some structure that helps to <u>memorize</u> it, the actual **Transfer of Learning** remains minimal. Regardless how excellent the material was.

Your Transfer of Learning is the key goal I have with my books. That's why they are all clearly structured.

Without some structure, we are likely to be <u>left confused when to apply what</u>. Meaning, we may (at best) remember a certain training technique of a great author or dog trainer, but we may apply it in the wrong situation! In a situation where it cannot yield success, and where we had better applied a different technique.

How is it with you? When you've applied a dog training technique that you learned from a great author or professional dog trainer, did your dog always react the way your dog was supposed to react? The way you expected?

And where the training didn't bear fruit, did you know why? Could you go back to the book or trainer and find out *why* your dog might react differently, and what you can do about it?

So when I realized that none of the dog training books on the market offer any systematization of their training approach, I felt that I had to devise some form of systematization myself.

To jog my own memory when to apply what, and to help my readers to jog their memory too, I distilled the elements of typical dog training situations. Let's call them **Tools**. Tools that systematically belong together, let's call **Toolset**. Given that there are so many of these Dog Training Tools, all of them together let's call **Toolkit**.

<u>This</u> is what's missing in all other dog training books:

A clearly defined set of Tools, plus advice and examples *when* and *how* to use them!

As I cannot easily memorize the entire **Toolkit** and its structure myself, I also built a <u>mindmap</u>. Given my age, all of this has tremendously helped to jog my memory. And so it should do for yours too.

So, with this book...

... for the first time in human history :-)

... I proudly present to you the

DOG TRAINING TOOLKIT

The DOG TRAINING TOOLKIT allows to train your dog much more effectively. And if you are a professional dog trainer, the Dog Training Toolkit allows you to advise dog owners much more professionally. Because now you can **explain why** a certain technique of yours will help or won't help in a given situation. And the dog owner can apply the same, and will yield the same result. And if the dog's situation is different, the owner now knows what to do instead. What a welcome change!

Indeed:

The DOG TRAINING TOOLKIT completely redefines all dog training in the world

- for those who make use of it! Practice is everything.

I believe that, with the Dog Training Toolkit:

- *All* dog owners can better train their dog, not just the expert dog trainers
- *All* dog owners are happier with their dog, so no dog ends up in the shelter (or worse!)
- *No* child is bitten anymore, because all parents can now show their children how to avoid it!

What an idealistic belief, I know - because this would require that all readers tell all others what they learned. You too.

The purpose of this book is to <u>introduce you</u> to the **Dog Training Toolkit**. For its application to numerous more dog training situations I have to refer to the **Adult Dog Behavior** <u>Training Compendium</u> (mygermanshepherd.org/go/training-compendium) - which is my next milestone - or, if you have or get a puppy, to the <u>Puppy Development Guide - Puppy 101: The Secrets to Puppy Training without Force, Fear, and Fuss</u> (mygermanshepherd.org/go/puppy-development-guide) - which is already available, and now in its 10th edition!

Dog Training Without Clear Tools Means Messing Around

I would argue that:

- *Without* having a **Dog Training Toolkit**, and knowing how to use it, we cannot successfully train our dog!

- Like an auto mechanic cannot repair our car if he doesn't have his toolkit and knows how to use it.

- Like we cannot build a house if we don't have a toolkit and know how to use it.

- Like a cook cannot prepare a delicious meal if she doesn't have her toolkit and knows how to use it.

Obviously, any such toolkit can never be considered complete. It will develop, like we - and our dogs - develop too.

Thanks to our (free) Periodical subscribers (mygerm anshepherd.org/my-german-shepherd/get-mygerma nshepherd-periodical-for-free) I receive constant feedback, and all feedback has been considered in this newest edition (you can see the edition number at the front of the book).

Please do send your feedback as well. I am not one of those hotshot authors who don't care about individual readers. I look after every reader - but don't you worry, it's not as many as the hotshot authors have, I still know everyone by name. ;-)

Who knows, maybe it is YOUR feedback that encourages me to publish a new edition soon?

Please send your feedback to support@mygerma nshepherd.org

Now you know where to look if later you seek to send an email.

How to Use This Book Best

Printing

I suggest you first print out the <u>Dog Training Toolkit Mindmap</u> shown in the next chapter (better after downloading it in full-size) and lay it next to you. This will allow you to see relationships between the dog training tools while you read. Thus it will significantly jog your memory and boost your transfer of learning, such that your dog quicker benefits from your new-found insight! :-)

Much later in the book you may also want to print out the <u>Commands Little Helper</u>, or you use it straight from the book, however you prefer.

Links

Throughout the entire book the focus is on helping you through relevant <u>links</u>, like we do on our breed rescue site <u>mygermanshepherd.org</u> - the largest such site in the world.

Book-internal links

The <u>abundance of cross-links</u> should allow you to use this **Dog Training Toolkit** as **reference guide**, moving around as you like.

Book-external links

Many of these links lead to <u>additional content for you</u>. Primarily to our (normally members-only) *Periodicals*, most of which are extensively researched and comprehensive discussions of a specific topic. That's why I decided to <u>link</u> the extra content, such that whenever you want, you can visit the linked webpages at your own choice to deepen your understanding.

Obviously, the linked Periodicals are <u>helpful to you regardless which breed of dog or mix you have</u> - *unless* we specifically state in one of those Periodicals that a certain point relates to the German Shepherd dog only. So, *do* make use of all the additional linked content, because they give you incredible more value above and beyond the limited space in this book. Okay?

All other external links are to <u>remedies</u> or articles on other websites. In case of remedy links, most of the time these point to Amazon, namely whenever Amazon offers the item and is the cheapest source (which is generally the case since they have the biggest buying power globally, and many vendors use Amazon as sales platform for their own items).

Note that the majority of dog products are being developed and marketed where the majority of pet dogs live: 78 million in the USA! Hence our default remedy links point to amazon.<u>com</u> - and I have done the same in this book. But what if you live in Canada, or you want to gift the item to your sister in the UK who has a dog too?

Then you would need to get the <u>ebook</u>, which uses cute flags to help you find the right item in any Amazon locale (so many links wouldn't be possible in a print book). Thus, instead of say:

<u>Nutramax Dasuquin with MSM</u> (mygermanshepherd .org/go/nutramax-msm) - which is without doubt the *top* remedy for dog mobility problems(!) -

...the ebook would show: <u>Nutramax Dasuquin with MSM</u> ▓▓ ▓▓ ▓▓ ▓▓ ▓▓ ▓▓ (like we do it on our website). The links embedded in each cute flag give ebook readers the freedom to choose their preferred supplier (I love freedom). Nice side effect: The flags also lighten up the text and they document that our world is increasingly interconnected - certainly for dogs.

"Dogs know no borders"

(Well, this is not entirely true, as you will see with the Dog Training Tool <u>Barrier</u>, p~68)

All links route through our site, this is how we can ensure that you get the *right* remedy: When a top remedy is no longer top, we replace the link on our site.

<u>Example</u>: Formerly the *Solvit* was the top car bench seat cover - until the vendor reduced the product quality to increase profit! When we heard this from our members (long before anyone posted it on Amazon), we simply replaced the link to point to the new top bench seat cover from *Formosa*. We have such a loyal fanbase because we try very hard to identify the BEST in everything!

Special Note for the Print Edition

Obviously with a print book the biggest disadvantage is that you cannot simply click on a linked word or image to jump to another book location, or to see the linked remedies, articles, or our site's Periodicals.

To give you access to the <u>book-internal cross-references and linked external extras</u> nonetheless, I have painstakingly added page numbers and web addresses (URLs) to the relevant text locations. Took me ages, but I expect it will help you enormously when you seek more detail in future. Just note that due to the print process the page references can get slightly off track. Okay?

The <u>URLs have hard line breaks</u>, so that you can type them exactly as you see them (just without the line break). Example: mygermanshepherd.org/go/st yptic-powder

Other than this all <u>hyphenation</u> in this book is done automatically by Microsoft Word.

Customary terms

Customary terms - including all here defined **Dog Training Tools** - I've written in <u>T</u>itle <u>C</u>ase (or more accurate: in <u>S</u>tart <u>C</u>ase). Hopefully this helps you to become familiar with the Tools more quickly.

Dog differences

In terms of <u>adult dog training</u>, there exist a few distinct differences depending on:

1. whether we have a resident adult dog that we have raised since puppyhood, or

2. whether we adopt an adult dog from a prior owner, or

3. whether we adopt an adult dog from a shelter.

There are differences because, contrary to what you may have read or heard elsewhere, dogs generally *do* have a good memory of their past experiences! Obviously some dog breeds better than others, and some dogs better than others although of the same breed or mix.

This already is the first point that may surprise you, because most dog books tell the ordinary reader that dogs only have a *short-term* memory. Or should this read: Most ordinary dog books tell the reader that dogs only have a short-term memory? ;-)

Well, I *won't* simply repeat what others have said because a lot of that is wrong. Whether it's about our dog's memory, or about chocolate that would kill our dog, or about different food requirements for puppy, adult, and senior dog, or one of the countless other wrongs that seem to find their way into almost every dog book - although many such claims lack substance all the way.

So, no, I try to only give you <u>results of research</u> - this means diligent observation, providing stimuli and interacting with dogs, and then again lots of diligent observation and *educated* interpretation. Such research is normally only done by scientists like myself, not by *bloggers* - that seem to have come to dominate the internet (and the ebook market).

This is the only way to actually find out something *new* about dogs, and about our relationship with dogs - rather than simply copying what each copier copied from another copier, who all copied from the first one who wrote that. If right or wrong, none of the copiers will ever figure out, and their readers neither!

If you already have a dog at home, you can find proof yourself immediately:

- Expose your dog to either some wonderful experience (say, make your dog find a meaty lamb bone in the back of your car - assuming (s)he loves meaty lamb bones), or

- Expose your dog to a nasty experience (say, empty a water bucket over your dog while it is dozing - I hope you won't(!), but that's all nastiness I could come up with).

In either case, wonderful or nasty experience, you will be able to notice that, from now on your dog will associate the <u>experienced environment</u> - or even the <u>overall situation</u> - with that very experience!

Say, your dog will from now on look and sniff for a meaty bone in the back of your car - and be scared, or even aggressive, when you approach your dog with a bucket (even if it's empty).

Your dog will remember either <u>environment</u> forever, or at least for many years to come! Possibly (s)he will even remember the <u>overall situation</u> - meaning, you might find your dog looking and sniffing for a meaty bone in *any* car, and be scared of *any* person approaching your dog with a bucket.

Further proof: A rescue dog that had no prior experience with you whatsoever (but often has had a great deal of other experiences with a prior owner and/or within the shelter), will at times reveal just that. There will be moments when you wonder: "Where did *that* now come from? Why does (s)he behave *that* way?".

The dog behaves that way because of memories of what had happened earlier in the dog's life - or what did not happen although it should have, like comprehensive socialization.

This may be:

- an inconspicuous matter like 'picking up a bucket'

- 'finding a meaty bone in the back of a car' (probably not)

- you turning on the vacuum cleaner

- your neighbor mowing the lawn

- you closing the kennel door

- you leaving your dog alone

- or whatever else!

Something that awakens your dog's memories or interferes with your dog's genetic instincts.

This doesn't mean that say a rescue dog brings so much 'luggage' that we don't know where to start unpacking. Because, we *do* know where to start unpacking. We do know what to do, and in which order, such that we get the dog we want. Even with the most difficult rescue dogs, oh yes!

Because this only requires genuine knowledge and...

Practice

When you subsequently study the dog training tools be aware that, depending on which dog you have or get (see 1, 2, and 3 above), you may need more or less <u>practice</u> to see how your dog reacts to the tools you use (same for me too, with every new dog).

The first step is to <u>understand the Tools</u> in this DOG TRAINING TOOLKIT. Read them many times, jump around as you like. The Toolkit has an abundance of cross-links for this very reason.

Then become familiar with the Tools: <u>Try them out</u>. Nothing can replace <u>practice</u>. Like for the auto mechanic, the builder, and the cook (see <u>Dog Training without clear Tools means messing around</u>, p~20).

That's what this **DOG TRAINING TOOLKIT** is about: Giving you a PRACTICAL TOOLKIT how you can <u>turn any dog into the dog you always wanted</u>, even the most difficult rescue dog.

Make your dog the dog that you will never want to give up on - because you *both* feel mutual love and happiness

This is my personal goal, both with our site and with my books: To do whatever I can to try **to help you being happier with your dog**. So that no more dogs end up in a shelter, or in a high-kill kennel, or

are being maltreated, or silently killed in the back-
yard.

―――――――――

Okay, now that we've made it as far as to the end of
the introduction, that's half of the book finished!

Just kidding :-)

<u>A final note just in case</u>:

If, despite *applying* the advice you just read (practice),
after a few weeks you still feel overwhelmed by the
amount of new content here, then take one step
back and <u>start easy</u>:

Both you and your dog will already be MUCH
happier once you <u>simply replace all force and fear
with *Collar Freeze* and *Isolation*</u>

(not hyperlinked so that you see the mindmap in the
next chapter first).

The DOG TRAINING TOOLKIT Mindmap

Like the book title promises, going forward you can use a PRACTICAL TOOLKIT to train your dog. Oh yeah!!

If you prefer the traditional style of dog training books - full of prose, poor in structure (and even poorer in terms of Transfer of Learning) - then this book may not be for you. Because this book is full of structure, which should allow a near 100% success rate for your Transfer of Learning - <u>if you want it</u>.

But if you **enjoy the difference**, then on the next page you see an image of a *mindmap* I created to show at a glance <u>selected Tools</u> from the **DOG TRAINING TOOLKIT** we are going to use.

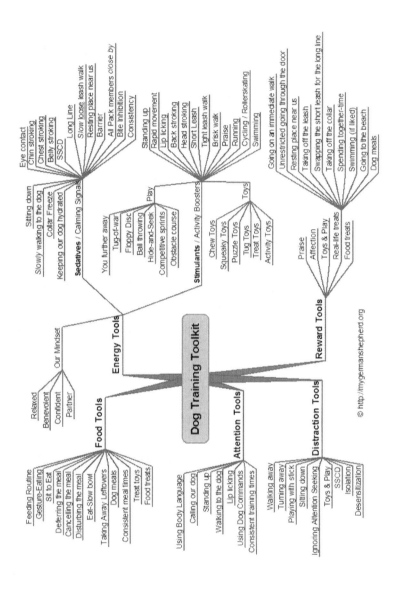

Dog Training Toolkit

Energy Tools

Our Mindset
- Relaxed
- Benevolent
- Confident
- Partner

Sedatives / Calming Signals
- Eye contact
- Chin stroking
- Chest stroking
- Belly stroking
- SSCD
- Long Line
- Slow loose leash walk
- Resting place near us
- Barrier
- All Pack members *close by*
- Bite Inhibition
- Consistency
- Sitting down
- Slowly walking to the dog
- Collar Freeze
- Keeping our dog hydrated

Stimulants / Activity Boosters
- You further away
- Play
  - Tug-of-war
  - Floppy Disc
  - Ball throwing
  - Hide-and-Seek
- Competitive sprints
- Obstacle course
- Standing up
- Rapid movement
- Lip licking
- Back stroking
- Head stroking
- Short Leash
- Tight leash walk
- Brisk walk
- Praise
- Running
- Cycling / Rollerskating
- Swimming

Toys
- Chew Toys
- Squeaky Toys
- Puzzle Toys
- Tug Toys
- Treat Toys
- Activity Toys

Reward Tools
- Praise
- Affection
- Toys & Play
- Real-life treats
- Food treats
- Going on an immediate walk
- Unrestricted going through the door
- Resting place near us
- Taking off the leash
- Swapping the short leash for the long line
- Taking off the collar
- Spending together-time
- Swimming (if liked)
- Going to the beach
- Dog meals

Food Tools
- Feeding Routine
- Gesture-Eating
- Sit to Eat
- Deferring the meal
- Cancelling the meal
- Disturbing the meal
- Eat-Slow bowl
- Taking Away Leftovers
- Dog meals
- Consistent meal times
- Treat toys
- Food treats

Attention Tools
- Using Body Language
- Calling our dog
- Standing up
- Walking to the dog
- Lip licking
- Using Dog Commands
- Consistent training times

Distraction Tools
- Walking away
- Turning away
- Playing with stick
- Sitting down
- Ignoring Attention Seeking
- Toys & Play
- SSCD
- Isolation
- Desensitization

© http://mygermanshepherd.org

With my eyes, I can't see the tools easily on this image, and maybe you neither. So, here's a <u>download link for you to get the mindmap</u> in case you'd like to have it: mygermanshepherd.org/kdp/forms/Dog-Training-Toolkit.pdf

No worries: You do *not* need to leave your email, like on other sites. To become a subscriber of our Periodicals is a *privilege*, we would never make it a requirement. And they aren't for everyone anyway.

Note though that the mindmap is *not* necessary in order to understand the Dog Training Toolkit. It's more like a backdrop that helps to orientate the mind - hence called <u>mindmap</u>.

To help you understand these many Tools when we discuss them subsequently, you may want to <u>print out the mindmap and lay it next to you</u>. This should make it much easier to follow my explanations and cross-references.

Thereafter, the best place for the mindmap?

Yep! Stick it on the fridge with some cute dog paw magnets, so that you keep looking at it: mygermansh epherd.org/go/paw-print-magnets

Note that this is just *our* **Dog Training Toolkit** at mygermanshepherd.org and for this book, obviously you could devise your own, now that you got the idea, ha! - Although I am not sure if different Tools or a different structure would serve you well...

To understand which Dog Training Tools are most effective for your dog in a given situation, guess what - you must first know the Tools, and then try out the Tools that you learned are most sensible in your situation.

That's what this Tooolkit is about:

- Showing you the Tools and how they work

- Encouraging you to practice using the Tools.

The Adult Dog Behavior Training Compendium will then discuss all pertinent dog training situations (if I ever get it ready). Like all my other books, it implies that you are familiar with the Dog Training Tools presented and explained in this book.

It is probably fair to say that once you know and understand this DOG TRAINING TOOLKIT, you will belong to the elite circle of the *best* educated dog owners and dog trainers in the world! You may even find yourself starting to train your friends' dogs once they notice how well you are in control of your own dog.

Now let's 'briefly' discuss our Toolkit, so that it becomes clearer *why* we will use certain Tools in certain dog training situations that we are going to discuss in future, and *how* they can help solve our 'dog problems'.

Energy Tools

A crucial point for every dog owner to understand is:

Canines are energy recipients

Meaning, dogs assume the dog owner's or handler's **energy state** easily. - By the way, humans are energy donors. Snakes, elephants, lions, and cats too (that's why your energy state has little influence on your success when you train your cat).

Whether we feel stressed or relaxed, excited or calm, sad or happy, mad or indifferent, amicable or confrontational, clearheaded or confused - our dog is likely to assume the same energy state within seconds.

This is in their genes. Dogs in the wild, as well as their ancestors (wolves), are not that high up in the food chain; although they have more below them than above, they have too many animals above them that would kill them in an instant if dogs weren't able to sense the energy level and the mood of their opponents (whether natural predators or not).

With our **domesticated dogs**, this is not just about the likelihood of an attack but about a whole range of feelings of the dog owner that might result in *benefiting* the dog in the next few minutes (eg getting a food treat), or *threatening* the dog (eg being beaten), or anything in between.

At mygermanshepherd.org none of us do dog training for a living, but the best of the professional dog trainers use an 'Energy Meter' to determine the **energy state** of any dog they work with (no electronic unit, but through *observing* the dog). So does Dan Abdelnoor (yes that 'Doggy Dan', the professional dog trainer with that awesome dog training video site).

Dan is still our favorite because he entirely relies on a *gentle* dog training approach like we do. And of course because his video site is such a great training instrument, and many of our dog-owning members express training needs, but don't want to pay big on a local trainer (for training methods they can't control, and results they can't replicate).

Regarding the **energy state** of a dog, Dan says that once a dog is midway through the Energy Meter (so above level 5, because it has 10 levels) it becomes next to impossible to teach the dog anything! And based on all our own experiences I can confirm this.

This is the reason why we hear dog owners complaining: "My dog doesn't listen to me!"

Can you relate?

Their dog *cannot* listen to them because the dog is mentally hyperactive, the dog is at an energy level above 5 - where *any* dog is becoming increasingly unresponsive, no matter how compliant the dog normally is.

The real issue however is that many dogs are almost *permanently* on a high energy level! The dog owner's behavior just doesn't allow the dog to switch off. This is critical, not only for health reasons (see later the Health Compendium) but also for behavior reasons:

A stressed dog is likely to become quickly an aggressive dog

Latent aggression can lead to that "sudden biting" we are familiar with from the news (at least!).

The <u>cause</u> of latent aggression is almost always that the dog is kept on a high energy level for far too long!

This explains the importance of using **Energy Tools** in our dog training approach, and this is why I feature them here first.

The next point for every dog owner to understand is that *anything* we want from our dog boils down to either:

- We want to get our dog **DO** something

- Or we want to get our dog **NOT** do something

If it's the first case - that we want to get our dog DO something - then we need to use Energy Tools that are <u>Stimulants</u>.

Conversely, if it's the second case - that we want to get our dog NOT do something - then we need to use Energy Tools that are **Sedatives**.

This equally applies to anyone else's dog we may encounter, say on the street or in the woods or wherever. To be <u>safe</u>, we MUST know how to use our Energy Tools. So yes, your children certainly should read this book too! Or read it to them. Or: Get the audio version.

Now you may be wondering: Why at all *Stimulants*, why would we want to get our dog DO something? Isn't it that we always want to get our dog NOT do something?

Not to bark, not to whine, not to jump up, not to dig, not to scratch our furniture, not to chew our shoes or whatever, not to occupy the couch or linger in our bed, not to bite, and oh what else not to!?

Well, that is correct if we only think of dog training as being <u>reactive</u>, ie to *correct* dog behavior. But I don't see it that way.

In my opinion, **<u>proactive</u> dog training is much better training**. In other words, to train our dog to behave in a way that does not lead to what we would perceive as 'dog problems' - standard dog behavior that <u>we</u> consider as a problem.

The benefits of being proactive will become most evident when you consider the <u>complete House Training guide</u> (House Training Dogs to Behave Well in a High Value Home: mygermanshepherd. org/go/house-training-guide) - because clearly, with all components of <u>House Training</u> we want to be *proactive* - to avoid a mess in our house!

But before we use Stimulants, let's first discuss <u>Sedatives</u>.

Sedatives

Sedatives help us to get our dog (or anyone's dog) NOT do something. They *calm down* the dog.

Many dog experts refer to Sedatives as **Calming Signals**, but Calming Signals are merely a *subset* of **Sedatives**.

Actually, more than a few dog experts have only looked at Calming Signals that <u>dogs</u> use, but of course we too can (and should) use Calming Signals when we interact with dogs - both with our own dog and (particularly!) with dogs we meet on the street.

Also note that some **Calming Signals** require a certain execution in order to be calming to the dog - else they may actually rather *upset* the dog. Likewise, some **Sedatives** are *not* Calming Signals (not a signal at all), still they have a calming effect on the dog - regardless whether we are signaling anything.

This will become clearer when we briefly discuss some Sedatives subsequently:

Sitting down

<u>Sitting down</u> is a Calming Signal to our dog. When we sit down, our energy level drops. Since dogs are energy recipients, our dog's energy level will drop too. With a small delay, it will drop as much or as little as our own energy level drops.

Similarly, making <u>our dog</u> **sit down** (<u>SIT Command</u>, p~193) is a **Sedative** as well, but it is not a Calming Signal. Because we aren't signaling anything with our own behavior, we are giving a <u>Dog Command</u> (p~191) instead.

So right here with the *first* Dog Training Tool we already understand a crucial difference between the traditional **Obedience Training** and our proprietary **Behavior Training**:

Why use *Commands* when we can use *Tools*?

Using Dog Commands is just 1 of 87 Tools of our Dog Training Toolkit! So why do so many dog owners (and worse: dog trainers!) focus solely on dog commands? I don't get it.

A concise introduction into the differences between the traditional **Obedience Training** and our proprietary **Behavior Training** you can find in the complete House Training guide (mygermanshepherd .org/go/house-training-guide) - a highly recommendable book that should come with every dog.

So: **Use more Tools and less Commands**, and you will have a much better relationship with your dog! Your dog will LOVE you for it.

Here: Instead of commanding SIT, just sit down yourself (or use one of the other **Sedatives**). This will calm down your dog much more than when you *command* the dog to calm down - because then the dog is experiencing a *conflict* in the Pack (this is the PRIME SECRET about Dogs, explained in the Puppy Development Guide (mygermanshepherd.org /go/puppy-development-guide) as well as in the House Training guide mentioned above).

Plus, it will save your <u>Dog Commands</u> (p~191) for when you need them. Because the *less* commands you use, the more impact they will have *when* you eventually use them!

Makes sense, hm? Exactly! But then why are so many dog trainers and dog owners *besotted* with the command-heavy Obedience Training?!

This is not a book about Obedience Training, but if you want to know the answer, see this Periodical on our site: mygermanshepherd.org/periodical/obedience-training-pros-and-cons. Once you read that, you *will* think twice how you train your dog. Oh yes!

The key never is what we <u>know</u>, the key always is what we <u>do</u>!

At mygermanshepherd.org we do <u>Behavior Training</u>, ie we behave in a way that motivates the dog to behave the way we want. Because Behavior Training beats Obedience Training in every regard - as you will notice when you try out the tools for some time.

Walking to the dog

<u>Walking to the dog</u> *can* be a Calming Signal (but often it is not). Only if we walk *very slowly* to our dog, it will have a calming effect on the dog. If we approach the dog a tad too quickly, it may instead either scare or confuse the dog, or invade its assumed territory without invitation.

The *speed* of movement significantly determines a dog's interpretation of that movement

Unless you are new to dogs, you will know that canines have a much larger Comfort Zone than humans (with animals, it's typically called Territory). If you invade their assumed Territory without invitation, some dogs (like some people!) get <u>very angry</u> (called Territorial Aggression).

So what's an **invitation** from a dog's viewpoint?

To have a good chance to be *invited* into a dog's assumed Territory, freeze for a moment, briefly look in the dog's eyes, and lightly bow (at least a bit the head down, while keeping the dog in your field or vision, for safety).

This gives a good chance to be *invited*, but obviously cannot give a guarantee for every dog in every situation. Some dogs simply may not *want* to invite you in a certain environment or situation, or at a certain time.

You need to detect this from the **dog body language**. I really can't go into any more detail in this book, but here's a leading photographic guide on canine body language (mygermanshepherd.org/go/canine-body-language).

Collar Freeze

The **Collar Freeze** is the best Calming Signal of all - it calms down ourselves too. :-)

The Collar Freeze we use for <u>lighter misconduct</u> - say, our dog is chewing our shoes for the first time, or scavenging an item outside, or barking for no acceptable reason (from the canine viewpoint there is always a good reason, but *we* may not accept it).

What is the Collar Freeze?

Upon lighter misconduct of our dog (misconduct in our view), we calmly <u>walk to</u> the dog and we *gently* take hold of our dog's <u>collar</u> (mygermanshepherd. org/go/bestselling-leather-collar), with one hand, on the *outer underside* - not at the neck or throat!

We simply <u>hold</u> the collar, nothing else

Now <u>we freeze</u>: We stand still, we don't speak to the dog, we don't touch, and we don't look either. We breathe deeply, we appreciate that we are alive and have a dog, and that we got this book... - We transmit our low energy to our dog.

In fact, initially our dog will *look at us* (all dogs do in this situation), but after a while (s)he will no longer look up at us, and that's the first indication that our dog is finally:

- calming down

- understanding that its behavior wasn't what we wanted

- and somehow 'saving a marker' in memory that seems to prevent repetition (immediately or soon).

Some dogs require the **Collar Freeze** several times for the same misconduct before 'it sinks in', other dogs 'get the message' with the first Collar Freeze.

The speed of learning not only depends on the breed and specific dog, it also depends on <u>how we do it</u>: **The more apathetic, the better** (note what I highlighted above: We don't speak to the dog, we don't touch, and we don't look either).

<u>We freeze</u> until we feel that our dog is entirely calm and relaxed. This may take a minute or five minutes, but it's time well spent: It not only calms down our dog, it is incredibly relaxing for ourselves too! Maybe

that's *why* it calms the dog: Dogs are energy recipients, see the introduction to <u>Energy Tools</u> (p~39) above. You deserve these breaks. Take them, and enjoy them. :-)

Keeping our dog hydrated

Keeping our dog hydrated is *not* a Calming Signal but nonetheless is a **Sedative** (so you see again, Calming Signals are really just a subset of Sedatives, p~45).

Hydration is a live-or-die factor for canines because dogs don't have 2 sq m or 21 sq ft of sweat gland covered skin (they have only minimal sweat glands at the paws). A well hydrated dog is much calmer than the dog would otherwise be (and without us having to signal anything).

So, both for health and behaviour reasons do make sure that you fill at least two drinking bowls (mygermanshepherd.org/go/spill-proof-dog-travel-bowl) with fresh water throughout the entire day! Even on cold days, where we ourselves might not desire to drink much apart from hot tea or coffee, we *must* supply sufficient fresh water, so that our dog can keep well hydrated.

One bowl should be right next to the dog's crate (also a great motivator to voluntarily retreat to the crate, see the House Training Guide), and another bowl could be right at our dog's favorite Resting Place during the day (p~66).

Eye Contact

Eye Contact is another of those Sedatives (p~45) that *can* be a Calming Signal to our dog (but often it is not). Only if we seek eye contact the *right* way, it will be calming to the dog (*how* we look, and *how long* we look).

As there is a seemingly unlimited range of ways *how* we can look when we seek eye contact with a dog (or indeed a human being), a general tip will be more helpful than even a set of example photos could be (and I could not shoot any anyway as I am bedridden):

A smiling face automatically changes the way we look to a friendly, unintimidating look. Yes, for dogs too - *unless* we use a smile which opens our mouth and shows our teeth (which we shouldn't do with a dog).

> When you smile to a dog,
> keep your mouth closed

So when you seek eye contact with a dog in order to *calm down* the dog (to get the dog NOT do something), add a <u>mild smile</u> - or give your eyes the appearance of <u>being tired</u> (lids falling half down).

Both these forms of eye contact are *calming* on a dog (the second more than the first). As always, *unless* your own energy level is hyper - because dogs are ...?

Yes! Dogs are <u>energy recipients</u> (p~39), you got it :-)

Chin Stroking

First note that, as a general rule, when we touch a dog from *below* its eye level then it is <u>calming</u> to the dog. When we touch a dog from *above* its eye level then it's likely to be <u>stimulating</u> (or even upsetting) the dog.

That's why you and particularly your children (let them read this!) should never stroke a dog they meet on the head or back (as most people wrongly do).

If you feel you can dare to stroke a dog (anyone's dog) under the chin, then do just that, and it will be <u>calming</u> to the dog. - If you feel you can't dare that, then that's a good indicator that it's probably safer *not* to stroke the dog at all!

And certainly it's more humane (ahem, canine), because if the dog doesn't *like* to be stroked, then why should we do it?!

Meaning, I don't like to argue with "don't get bitten", instead I prefer to argue with:

Do things <u>canines</u> like, not things humans like

Then we won't get bitten anyway!

Just because we can't see signs of distress doesn't mean the dog doesn't *feel* signs of distress. Many dogs are very subtle with the display of their true feelings.

Even more so, many dog owners cannot read canine body language - nor human body language (canine body language guidance I mentioned already (p~50), and the leading guide on human body language is from Allan Pease: mygermanshepherd.org/go/human-body-language). There is no guide yet available that teaches human body language towards dogs, but I am working on such a guide).

Chest Stroking

Similarly, when we stroke the chest of a dog from the *front* then we touch from *below* the eye level, so that's <u>calming</u> to the dog.

Note however that if we reach from the side (ie *behind* the front legs, like most people do) then it's likely to be *not* calming to the dog, unless we bend down to consciously reach out our hand *below* the dog's eye level.

In addition, we would need to make sure that the dog can see when we reach out to its side.

Belly Stroking

Obviously belly stroking comes always from the side (we won't grab through the hind legs, would we?), so that's the same issue as above:

To be sure it's a Calming Signal to the dog, we need to bend down so much that we can consciously reach out from *below* the dog's eye level.

And we need to verify that the dog's head is turned towards us enough such that our hand is visible when we reach out.

SSCD

SSCD stands for Start - Stop - Change Direction.

This is a fundamental Calming Signal that's helpful in countless situations when we have a <u>Short Leash</u> (mygermanshepherd.org/go/teaching-lead) available.

How SSCD works

1. Attach a short lead to your dog's collar

2. Start to walk slowly in one direction

3. Stop when you want, or when your dog *pulls* (in any direction!)

4. Change Direction

Repeat **SSCD** for a few minutes, or until your dog is totally calm: Always start to walk slowly in one direction, then stop whenever you want or when your dog pulls (in any direction), and then turn to change direction. It's really that easy!

Ways to use SSCD

We can do SSCD both indoors and outdoors, and it can serve four purposes:

- Sedative (p~45)

- Distraction Tool (p~200)

- Leash Training (mygermanshepherd.org/go/ leash-training-guide)

- Behavior Modification (a lot already in here)

And yes, **SSCD** is significantly relaxing for a dog! *Unless* of course, we are stressed ourselves.

While SSCD is so easy that a five-year old boy can do it, SSCD is a magically effective Dog Training Tool!

Long Line

Surprisingly *few* dog owners have a <u>Long Line</u> at all. This is surprising because a Long Line is an essential Dog Training Tool. If you don't have a Long Line, don't be surprised if you face dog training problems!

The best Long Line (in our view, and based on the feedback from thousands of dog owners) is the <u>Long Line</u> (mygermanshepherd.org/go/long-line) from Sarah Hodgson: Feather-light, robust, and gliding well over the ground, ie without the dog feeling it being much of a hindrance (exactly as it should be).

The freedom to run around while being on a Long Line is *calming* to dogs. The Long Line is a **Sedative**, but no Calming Signal.

Leash Walk

<u>Leash Walk</u> is another of those **Sedatives** that *can* be a Calming Signal (but often it is not). Only if we walk *really slowly* and with a short but *loose* leash, it will be calming on our dog.

Most dog owners I've seen on the street or in dog training lessons, on hikes or wherever, can neither walk slowly (because they are always in a hurry - on a high energy level!) nor can they walk their dog on a loose leash.

In such case, Leash Walking is a <u>Stimulant</u> (p~78).

Complete Leash Training guidance (incl. off-leash safety, heeling, the Recall etc) is in the <u>Leash Training guide</u> (mygermanshepherd.org/go/leash-training-guide).

Resting Place near us

Many perceived 'dog problems' result from the simple fact that the dog doesn't have its dedicated Resting Place near the dog owner.

If you feel that your dog is hyperactive in the house or during Leash Walk (p~74), then give this matter some consideration.

In *every* room where we linger in the house and where we want our dog to be with us, we need to make sure that our dog has its dedicated **Resting Place** near us.

This can be as simple and hard as throwing a blanket on the floor, or as caring and soft as a special dog nap mat (mygermanshepherd.org/go/westpaw-nap-blanket) or even a super comfy bumper bed (my-germanshepherd.org/go/westpaw-gsd-bumper-bed).

But if you *don't* provide these dedicated **Resting Places**, then don't be surprised if your dog occupies your couch instead, is stressed, follows you everywhere, and suffers Separation Anxiety!

And if you don't provide *comfy* Resting Places, then don't be surprised if your dog gets sore elbows, joint pain, and potentially even skin problems (for more see later the <u>Health Compendium</u>).

Barrier

A Barrier is *not* a Calming Signal but nonetheless a Sedative (p~45). It's only needed in certain situations: Where we want to restrict our dog's access to an area of concern.

For example, when we have a small or young dog *and* a staircase in the house (or any other area where our dog could fall down). In such cases we may want to put up a **Barrier**.

Barriers where nothing happens behind it (so where the behind doesn't raise our dog's attention), should be *opaque*. Good examples are this wooden fence/gate (mygermanshepherd.org/go/wooden-fence) or this wooden privacy screen (myger-manshepherd.org/go/wooden-privacy-screen).

Barriers where at times family action is behind it, should be *transparent* to be relaxing - so that our dog can see what's going on and doesn't feel totally excluded from its Pack, when all we want is to keep our dog safe. Good examples are this bamboo gate (mygermanshepherd.org/go/bamboo-gate) or this metal walk-through safety gate (mygermanshepherd.

org/go/safety-gate), and of course this banister shield (mygermanshepherd.org/go/banister-shield).

Indeed, in case you are in the situation mentioned, a transparent banister shield is indispensable.

Note that a **Barrier** can be as simple as a piece of self-adhesive tape put on the floor, or a ribbon spanning across two poles. Using bright yellow or bright blue is best because that's the visible canine color spectrum (see what your dog sees at my-germanshepherd.org/periodical/gsd-eye-care).

In many cases such a simple 'transparent' barrier is all that's needed to keep our dog out, while allowing the dog to see what's going on behind it. The chapter *How to Train Our Dog to Stay Out of the Kitchen - or Any Other Place* in the House Training guide already showed how to train our dog to *respect* such a Barrier.

All Pack members close by

All Pack members close by is a Sedative too (p~45). It will make our dog much calmer, because the next crucial point to understand is:

> **Domesticated dogs are more than just 'Pack animals' - they genetically *crave* to belong to a Pack!**

Very different to humans: While we too need social interaction, we can live fairly well *without* belonging to a (family) Pack - indeed, some of us *have* to live alone, and others *choose* to live alone. Neither will make us necessarily destructive or aggressive (in fact many who *choose* this lifestyle choose it because it gives them peace).

Conversely, domesticated dogs become *very* destructive and aggressive when they are excluded from a Pack structure. This is because we have bred the 'social factor' into the domesticated dogs for *at least* 50,000 dog generations!

To **understand the significance** consider this: Even since the *earliest* 'humans' (the proto Neanderthals), we humans have had only about *half* that number of generations - and thus gene mutation and social modification!

<u>This</u> is the reason why most of today's domesticated dogs <u>look and behave</u> so very different than their ancestors, the wolves. And why we humans resemble the proto Neanderthals still so much more. Certainly all "Creationists" should read this to understand the world.

Anyway, this is the reason why our domesticated dogs genetically *crave* for social interaction with us humans. And when we deny that social interaction, we seed 'dog problems' because it upsets our dog.

Conversely, when all Pack members are close by, it is calming for our dog. All Pack members close by is a **Sedative**.

Bite Inhibition

Like Desensitization (p~224), Bite Inhibition is more an overall training goal than an individual Dog Training Tool, because it actually requires us to use any number and combination of Tools of the Dog Training Toolkit presented in this book.

Bite Inhibition is a Sedative (p~45), because it limits the dog's energy level in both situations Bite Temptation and Bite Reflex.

The term 'Bite Inhibition' was coined by Ian Dunbar in his book After you get your puppy (mygermansh epherd.org/go/book-after-you-get-your-puppy). Bite Inhibition means:

- to limit the occurrence of biting, and

- to limit the bite force when bitten.

As explained in the Puppy Development Guide - Puppy 101, puppies learn this already from mum and litter mates during Litter Socialization, and it is wise to continue this training during Family Socialization and beyond, as an adult dog. Because this is our only guarantee to prevent significant injury from dog bites.

Bite Inhibition teaches our dog that (s)he has to be at least as careful with us human Pack members as (s)he had to be with the canine Pack members during puppyhood.

The four most important opportunities for **Bite Inhibition training** are when we give Meals (p~168) or Food Treats (p~141), during Play (p~104), when we swap Toys (p~132), and during Mouth Care (later in the Care Compendium):

- Briefly taking away the food bowl

- Briefly interrupting meals to add a tasty morsel

- Hand-feeding morsels

- Play-fighting - with frequent controlled inter-ruptions!

- Taking away a bone, chew toy, and other toys from the mouth

- Toothbrushing and mouth inspection

When used consistently, these measures train our dog both:

- to *consciously* limit <u>Bite Temptation</u> and <u>Bite Force</u>

- and to *subconsciously* develop a modified <u>Bite Reflex</u>.

For more detail see in the <u>Training Compendium</u> later (mygermanshepherd.org/go/training-compend ium) the chapter *How to train our dog not to bite*.

Consistency

Consistency is a Dog Training Tool because it dramatically accelerates our dog training success. Indeed, in many cases **Consistency** is a prerequisite for training success.

This is not limited to using the same Dog Commands (p~191), hand cues and other Body Language (p~179), tone of voice, etc. Consistency is also very helpful in terms of Training Times (p~198), Meal Times (p~169) and overall Feeding Routine (p~145).

Consistency is a Sedative (p~45) because it is calming for a dog. Dogs thrive on consistency, they love routine.

Interestingly dogs don't get as easily bored as we do. You can throw a ball 20 times, and a healthy dog will run to fetch the ball like it was the first time ever. Same motivation, same excitement, same spirit!

Stimulants

Now on to Stimulants! Stimulants help us to get a dog DO something. They *encourage* the dog.

Stimulants can range from *gentle* stimulation of our dog's energy state to full-blown activity boosters: exercise.

Standing Up

Standing Up is a **Stimulant** to our dog. When we stand up, our energy level rises. Since dogs are energy recipients, our dog's energy level will rise too. With a small delay, it will rise as much or as little as our own energy level rises.

Rapid Movement

When we move our arms or our entire body *rapidly*, we draw a lot energy for this physical activity - we *raise* our energy level. If our dog is close by and notices our rapid movement, it will send him or her in alarm state - (s)he will instantly be on high energy too.

As mentioned earlier, the **speed** of movement significantly determines a dog's interpretation of that movement. Thus, if we are worried that our dog (or anyone's dog!) might misinterprete our speedy movement, then we better move much calmer!

For example, in some situations most dogs can completely misinterprete the rapid movements of children. The high energy *immediately* puts them on high energy too. The problem:

A *quick* change in energy level up the scale
is likely to cause aggression in dogs!

This is the reason why not only many children are being attacked by dogs, but also why so many postmen, cyclists, joggers and the like are being attacked by dogs.

To deliver all the letters they have in their bag, postmen put on an enormous speed in their step and in their arm movements. When they approach your house this way, your dog instantly assumes the postman's high energy level - and boom! you have an aggressive dog - one that may otherwise be the most docile dog in the world.

So, **rapid movement** is somewhat a 'dangerous' Stimulant (p~86): We must be able to scale it depending on the dog's reaction.

Lip Licking

First note that the most fundamental quest of any dog is to <u>secure food</u> (unless the dog is traumatized).

This is a genetic quest of *all* dogs, because dogs (even our domesticated dogs) don't quite know if and when they get their next meal. Particularly not, if we don't stick to <u>Consistent Meal Times</u> (p~169). Dogs notice the slightest variations here.

Dogs are fully aware that they, and we, use the *mouth* for food intake. - If you doubt anything relating to dog consciousness, a great book on the consciousness of canines is <u>The Intelligence of Dogs: Canine Consciousness and Capabilities</u> (mygermanshepherd. org/go/book-intelligence-of-dogs-consciousness) from Stanley Coren.

So when our dog watches us **Lip Licking**, (s)he suspects that something very important is going on or is going to happen soon. This lifts our dog rapidly onto a high energy level.

Since a *quick* change in energy level <u>up</u> the scale is likely to cause **aggression**, we now better have something great in mind that we plan to do - or we may soon see the first signs of aggression.

Back Stroking

As explained under <u>Sedatives</u> (p~45), the common back stroking is actually <u>not</u> a nice thing to do, because here we touch the dog from *above* its eye level, and this may upset the dog if (s)he feels frightened or threatened.

━━━━━━━━━━━━━━━━━━

How often have we seen this scene:

An adult or a child meets a dog owner with dog on the street. The dog is well-behaved (well-trained) and stays calm and somewhat aloof.

The adult or child wants the dog to be more responsive (affectionate) and approaches the dog and strokes its back. In an instant the dog gets very agitated and the dog owner has to restrain the dog with the leash.

━━━━━━━━━━━━━━━━━━

Back stroking certainly is a <u>Stimulant</u> (even if the dog remains still), but it does not necessarily make the dog more active in the way we want!

Head Stroking

<u>Head stroking</u> is an even stronger <u>Stimulant</u> than back stroking. Head stroking is likely to upset the dog, especially when we *pat* on the head.

Have someone pat on *your* head, and you will know how that feels. And now consider that the human skull is much harder than the canine skull. So patting a dog's head really gives a terrible 'knock-knock' feeling.

I bet all children hate their head being stroked, I certainly did. With another person's dog, I strongly advise children and adults *against* head stroking.

Once you have a good bonding with your own dog and (s)he trusts you, you can of course safely stroke the head. Nonetheless, the question again is, why *do* something that our dog likely won't like? Just because (s)he bears it, doesn't mean (s)he appreciates it, right?

Short Leash

The Short Leash (mygermanshepherd.org/go/teach ing-lead) is a **Stimulant** (p~78), because upon seeing the leash the dog knows from experience that we are going to attach the leash to the collar that is around the dog's *neck*.

No dog likes to be pulled around at its neck! Depending on how much you (or a prior dog owner or handler) have done just that, your dog may get very agitated from merely *seeing* the Short Leash.

This is why for many dogs the Short Leash is upsetting. Nonetheless a loose-leash walk can be calming - see Leash walk (p~65) under Sedatives (p~45) above.

A lot depends on using the *right* collar and the *right* leash, and then of course introducing the dog to the short leash the *right* way. For more details see the Leash Training guide (mygermanshepherd.org/go/ leash-training-guide).

Since many dog owners realize that they have introduced their dog to the Short Leash the *wrong* way, at the end of this book you will find how to

<u>Desensitize</u> (p~224) a dog from past experience or instinct, such that you can re-introduce *any* item the *right* way (including the **Short Leash**).

Tight Leash Walk

Almost all dog owners walk their dog on a *tight* leash - and in some cases it looks like the dog is walking the dog owner. ;-)

The tight leash walk is stimulating the dog towards a higher energy level. In fact, long and repetitive experience of a tight leash causes aggression in a dog. So then why do so many dog owners walk their dog on a tight leash?

Because the dog owners are on a high energy level themselves! They are stressed from all the commitments in their daily life: problems in the job (or no job), problems in the family, mortgage and credit card debts, an empty bank account, etc.

They can't calm down. They can't let go of the pressure. So when they walk their dog, they can't let go of their dog either. Not even beyond the length of the leash. Yes, not even one meter.

But because of their own stress level, they can't train their dog to heel either. Hence, more often than not, they accept to be dragged behind - or, if the dog is small, the dog has to accept to be *pulled* most of the way.

So now *three* <u>Stimulants</u> (p~78) for the dog come together:

- being tied to the neck!

- *and* all the distractions in the environment

- *and* assuming all the energy from their owner

This is too much for any dog: A tight leash walk can elevate a dog to level 7, 8, or even 9 on <u>Dan's Energy Meter</u> (mygermanshepherd.org/go/online-dog-trainer) - and thus can lead to aggression!

When I meet dogs outdoors on a <u>tight leash</u> - whether dragging their owner behind or seemingly sniffing calmly in the bushes, I carefully keep a great distance. Because I anticipate that the dog's energy state may be dangerous for a stranger like myself.

Brisk Walk

This group of dog owners is very small, nonetheless once a while we can see these dog walkers who manage to walk their dog on a <u>loose leash</u> (because the dog heels very well), but - or should it read because? - they walk so *brisk* that it looks like their dog struggles to keep up.

The brisk walk means the dog owner is under high energy. And this means that the dog is assuming the high energy too (because dogs are energy recipients, see right under <u>Energy Tools</u> above, p~39).

But the brisk walk *consumes* a lot of this energy. Thus I would argue that a brisk walk cannot elevate a dog's energy to level 6 on the Energy Meter - like a <u>tight leash walk</u> easily will. In other words, a brisk walk is unlikely to make a dog aggressive.

However, a brisk walk doesn't *relax* the dog either! Nor the dog owner. Hence note that a brisk walk is *not* a recipe for a *calm loose leash walk*. A **brisk walk** is not calming the dog, it is **stimulating** the dog. It is *raising* the dog's energy state.

Praise

When we <u>praise</u> our dog, we typically change to a high-pitched, excited voice - we are on a higher energy level. Our dog assumes this energy and gets excited too. Praise is *not* a Calming Signal but a <u>Stimulant</u> (p~78).

The key point is that even when we feel we *reassure* our dog (say during a thunderstorm or in the midst of Halloween or New Year's firecrackers), to our dog this *sounds* like praise. So what we actually do in such moments is: We further *raise* our dog's energy level, we are not effectively calming down our dog.

<u>This</u> is why our reassurance in such situations has so little impact. Indeed, any little impact we notice solely derives from the fact that when we reassure our dog we are <u>Close to our dog</u> (p~70) - which is a <u>Sedative</u> (p~45), see above.

Conversely, the way we speak and act while we reassure, that's a <u>Stimulant</u>. The related crucial point to understand is:

<u>Stimulants</u> make the environment and situation *more* memorable, while <u>Sedatives</u> make it *less* memorable

Praise helps our dog to <u>memorize</u> the environment and situation, and associate it with the trained behavior.

<u>This</u> is why we may often feel that **Praise** allows for fast training success, but also why we need to <u>retrain</u> our dog in a *different* environment or situation when we used Praise as reward:

The Stimulant **Praise** made the particular environment and situation more memorable, and hence our dog may often relate the trained behavior to exactly that environment or situation - reducing the chance of *general* training success. (Even worse when we use <u>Food Treats</u> as reward)

Which leads to the next related crucial point to understand:

Canines cannot easily transfer trained behavior to new environments and situations

Dogs' <u>ability to abstract</u> is small. Which is why we normally have to train our dog the desired behavior in <u>multiple</u> environments and situations. - Or else we typically complain to our dog:

"Have you already forgotten what you learned yesterday??"

No, our dog has not forgotten, (s)he just doesn't feel that today's environment or situation has anything to do with yesterday's: We were on a different energy level (in a different mood), it was at a different time of day (between the dog meals), it was at a different place, it looked different, and most importantly it smelled different!

Hence the dog thinks:

"No I haven't forgotten yesterday, but what has yesterday to do with today??"

Running

Exercise, like making our dog <u>run</u>, obviously leads to a higher energy level. All exercise is stimulating. But the <u>outcome of exercise</u> is exhaustion, and that's a <u>Sedative</u> (p~45)!

This leads to the slightly irritating note that we can stimulate our dog with exercise when we want to *calm down* our dog.

Cycling/ Rollerskating

Subject to our dog's size and level of fitness (and our own ability to cycle or rollerskate well!), these forms of exercise are amongst the best to stimulate a dog to exhaustion - and thus to make the dog calm.

A truly exhausted dog is totally calm: There comes zero barking, whining, jumping up, digging, scratching, chewing, biting or other form of aggression from an exhausted dog! Zero.

This is why **working dogs** (herding, retriever, search and rescue, etc) generally are so much better behaved and less aggressive than say terriers and toy breed dogs: Their metabolism is geared to endurance (long stretches of physical exercise), while the metabolism of say terriers and toy breed dogs is geared to sprints (short bursts of activity).

So there is no need to argue with breed-specific predisposition to aggression, once we understand that most dog aggression is the result of stress, which is the result of high pent-up energy, which is the result of not using the right Energy Tools for the particular dog! More on this in just a moment.

Swimming

Swimming is another fantastic Stimulant (p~78) - IF your dog likes it (because not all dogs swim well and like swimming). On this note: Never force your dog to an activity (s)he doesn't like.

> Only mildly encourage your dog to try out
> a new activity (s)he may enjoy

Else you will outright *prevent* to see the blossoming of a great relationship with your dog! In addition, like with ourselves: Liking develops over time. Even what your dog doesn't like at say 6 years of age, (s)he may well learn to LOVE by say 9 years of age - IF you avoided force from the beginning.

Toys

When we want to *raise* our dog's energy level, we can also employ Toys. Toys are Stimulants (p~78).

So let's briefly discuss **Dog Toy Categories**. The examples here are arguably some of the TOP toys in each category:

> Chew Toys

Nylabone Galileo (mygermanshepherd.org/go/dog-chew-toys-nylabone-galileo) is an insanely tough nylon chew bone - great to strengthen a dog's teeth and gums, as well as providing something to release its energy level (and clean its teeth too).

Likewise, Westpaw's Hurley (mygermanshepherd. org/go/dog-chew-toys-hurley) is a super-tough, multi-functional chew bone that's ideal to be taken outside when you and your dog get some exercise, even in the water - because it floats.

> Activity Toys

Tail Teaser (mygermanshepherd.org/go/tail-teaser) is a new multi-purpose exercise toy for any dog and any age: You can use it both indoors and outdoors, and children can use it too. Maybe best of all: *We* don't need to exercise, we can stand still or even sit down - while the *dog* will get heavy exercise (if the dog is energetic), or mild exercise (if say the dog is old). Truly multi-purpose.

Likewise, Floppy disc (mygermanshepherd.org/go/dog-activity-toys-floppy-disc) is huge FUN and exercise for your dog (and for you too). It's better than the standard frisbee: Its floppiness is safer, healthier for teeth and gums, and it flies slower so that the dog can really see it close while chasing it. - Tip: Throw it to levitate ahead of and above your dog's reach! Cool!

Not just an **Activity Toy** but more like a full-blown autonomous exercise instrument for *strong* dogs(!) is the Varsity Ball (mygermanshepherd.org/go/varsity-ball). 100% indestructible, fairly heavy, and *safe* because it's non-disintegrating and too large to be swallowed.

The risk with the **Varsity Ball** rather is that some dogs get so carried away playing with this ball on their own for hours that they get *very* exhausted. Thus, without full <u>drinking bowls</u> (mygermanshep herd.org/go/spill-proof-dog-travel-bowl) nearby, we shouldn't let our dog play with this! And even then, initial observation is a *must* to gauge your dog's play-drive.

> Treat Toys

<u>Westpaw's Tux</u> (mygermanshepherd.org/go/dog-treat-toys-tux) is a great example. It's made of a non-toxic material trading as Zogoflex. Tux is pliable, bouncing, recyclable, buoyant, and dishwasher-safe too!

Likewise, <u>Kong Extreme</u> (mygermanshepherd.org/go/dog-treat-toys-kong-extreme). Maybe the tough-est non-toxic material of all, this buoy-shaped interactivity toy is perfect for the mental and physical stimulation of strong chewers. You can even place your dog's favorite treat inside and watch how (s)he tries to get at it while having FUN on its own with tossing around the buoy.

> Squeaky Toys

<u>Hartz Roundabouts</u> (mygermanshepherd.org/go/ dog-squeaky-toys-hartz-roundabouts) is a great example of squeak-only toys. They are made of latex that lasts.

Note though that you can't make every dog happy with squeaky toys - some dogs find them disturbing or annoying (I do too). But it's worth to try out one of these toys as well.

> Puzzle Toys

<u>Hide-a-Squirrel</u> (mygermanshepherd.org/go/dog-puzzle-toys-hide-a-squirrel) is immensely popular among mid-sized to large dogs. *Surprisingly* I'd say, because it's plush and it contains small parts (the squirrels).

Likewise, <u>Dog Egg-Babies</u> (mygermanshepherd.org /go/dog-puzzle-toys-egg-babies) is another multi-functional toy that promises your dog loads of lasting FUN, as well as mental and physical stimulation. Just don't get those with small, floppy parts (like eg the hedgehog has on its feet), then they last longer and are safer!

Note that these toys also squeak - as long as they work. ;-)

If money is not your prime concern then you may even want to consider <u>Nina Ottosson's wooden dog puzzle treat toys</u> (mygermanshepherd.org/go/wooden-dog-puzzle-toys). Indeed, they combine the benefits of sophisticated puzzle toys with treat toys, which is probably the most enjoyed alternative to outdoor exercise.

> Tug Toys

Most Tug Toys perform poorly, and it's better to just take a strong leather lead or cotton rope. However, one toy that isn't actually promoted as Tug Toy does have its merits:

<u>Fresh-N-Floss</u> (mygermanshepherd.org/go/dog-tug -toys-fresh-n-floss) is tough enough for a short, quick pull with the dog, and while doing so it is proven to be brilliant on the dog's teeth - while gentle enough for its gums.

A good alternative is Vip's Tuffy's Ultimate (my germanshepherd.org/go/dog-tug-toys-tuffys-ultimate). A soft Tug Toy of enormous strength with good oral cleaning effect.

Each of these six **Dog Toy Categories** stimulate dogs in different ways (senses involved, agility of different body parts, areas of mental motivation, etc).

I suspect that in terms of raising a dog's energy level, the following hierarchy seems to apply in general:

1. Treat Toys

2. Puzzle Toys

3. Activity Toys

4. Tug Toys

5. Squeaky Toys

6. Chew Toys

Chew Toys likely increase a dog's energy level least, and **Treat Toys** most.

Play

Lastly, <u>Play</u> offers unlimited opportunities to <u>stimulate</u> our dog, eg:

- Hide-and-seek

- Ball throwing

- <u>Floppy disc play</u> (p~95)

- Obstacle course

- Competitive sprints

- <u>Tug-of-war</u> and similar play-fighting (p~104)

- Play with <u>Puzzle Toys</u> (p~97)

- Discovery competitions (eg in <u>Treat Toys</u>), etc

Important to understand is though:

<blockquote>

**What determines a dog's energy level is not
the extent of physical exhaustion
but the dog's <u>mental state</u>**

</blockquote>

Even a dog that is standing transfixed can be on a high energy level. Indeed so high, that in the next split of a second the dog may bite!

So what the <u>energy level</u> actually is about,
is the <u>extent of unreleased energy</u>

And unreleased energy is entirely mental, not physical. You can aim to *release* pent-up energy through physical exercise (and that's wise), but if you don't address the **mental cause** of the pent-up energy then the problem will recur.

<u>This</u> is the reason why so many dog owners (and dog trainers!) fail to truly eliminate say biting issues with their dog. Worse: This is the reason why even dogs that have successfully completed *professional* dog training later suddenly show a wide range of behavior problems, including aggression.

Back to the <u>Stimulant</u> **Play**:

Any Play where we are *separated* from our dog
is likely to raise the dog's energy level *most*

Because, other matters being equal (which rarely they are!), the <u>further away</u> we are from our dog, the higher the dog's energy level will rise: Being separated from its Pack involuntarily *upsets* a dog (some sooner, others later) - due to the inherited quest to belong to a Pack (see the Tool All Pack members close by, p~70).

This applies to both Pack member and Pack leader, so even when we are not yet our dog's accepted Pack leader. The importance of *acceptance* will be discussed in *The Prime Secret about dogs* in the Training Compendium (or if you have the Puppy Development Guide - Puppy 101, it's in there too).

Thus, with Play like **Hide-and-seek**, the better we are at it (ie the more difficult we make it for our dog to find us), the more it will normally *raise* our dog's energy state while our dog cannot find us.

If we make it too difficult, it may even *upset* our dog to the degree of becoming irritated and nervous - at least level 5 on Dan's Energy Meter (mygermanshep herd.org/go/online-dog-trainer), where it starts to get critical with a dog.

All the above makes clear that when we use Energy Tools (p~39) or any other Dog Training Tools, we target the dog's mental state - even when we choose to exercise our dog to exhaustion in order to calm down our dog.

This is important to always remember:

With all **Dog Training Tools** we target the dog's mental state

So, even when during an engaging Tug-of-war our dog fletches its teeth and seems to get really agitated, I would argue that its energy level stays way below the one that our dog reaches when we throw a ball far away and our dog runs to fetch it - because this *separates* our dog from us, its Pack.

Obvious exception: If you have a dog that gets *aggressive* when during Tug-of-war you pull harder than (s)he does. But in such case you shouldn't be playing Tug-of-war at all!

Note on Tug-of-War and similar Play-Fighting

In *many* (cheap copy & paste) sources for dog training you can read the advice <u>not</u> to play <u>Tug-of-war</u> with your dog - typically without any explanation *why*. This is downright bad advice, *unless* your dog gets aggressive during play - but then you should address the aggression, not stop playing!

It is *bad* advice because with an adult dog, **controlled Play-fighting** like Tug-of-war offers an almost unique opportunity to train <u>Bite Inhibition</u> (p~72). Another great opportunity is during the <u>Feeding Routine</u> (p~138). The third opportunity is during Mouth Care and other Dog Care (see the <u>Care Compendium</u>). And the fourth opportunity is when we swap <u>Toys</u> (p~ 94).

Crucial however is the word *controlled*: We must first have taught our dog specific <u>Commands</u> (p~191) that are essential to get the dog's attention during Play-fighting, so that we maintain control over our dog at all times.

Even in the heat of the moment, when the dog is on a high energy level (mentally very engaged), we must always be able to get our dog to <u>STOP</u> all Play-fighting **on cue or command**.

Note on Ball Throwing

Rarely, but sometimes we can observe a dog that is <u>not</u> immediately coming back to its owner after catching the ball thrown away. Have you seen this?

This is a good indicator that the owner and the dog have a **Pack issue**. Indeed, when we continue to observe them we can almost always clearly see further indicators that document a disturbed Pack relationship.

It's not just that the dog owner is <u>not</u> the *accepted* Pack leader. No, sometimes the presumed owner turns out <u>not</u> to be the dog owner at all, but a professional dog walker. Other times a conversation brings to light that the dog is traumatized.

In short: A healthy dog of an *accepted* Pack leader (owner) will catch a thrown ball and *immediately* return to its owner (but typically only bring the ball back *all the way* if trained). A *delayed* return of the dog is a pretty reliable indicator that something is wrong (which should be worked on rather quickly!).

Our Mindset

Lastly, I have arranged the <u>Mindset</u> under <u>Energy Tools</u> (p~39) because it is our mindset that determines our <u>own</u> energy state. And, whether willfully or subconsciously, we transfer our energy state to our dog because dogs are energy recipients.

<u>This</u> is why **Our Mindset** plays such a crucial role in dog training. Very different to say training a cat (cats are energy donors).

Therefore, any dog trainer and any dog training book that doesn't address <u>your</u> mindset, *fails* before you even started. No matter how great the trainer or book seems to be, **your Transfer of Learning** will be very limited indeed.

Our Mindset? <u>What Mindset</u>?

Relaxed

If we want a <u>calm dog</u>, a dog that:

- doesn't chew our shoes

- doesn't scratch our furniture

- doesn't push over our ming vase

- doesn't jump up on our guests

- doesn't bark for prolonged periods

- doesn't whine all day or night

- doesn't circle around us with a wagging tail like it has to help our house cleaner

- doesn't chase moving objects (rabbit, squirrel, motorbiker, etc)

- doesn't bite us or strangers or other dogs

...then we <u>must</u> be relaxed ourselves whenever we engage with our dog. There is no way around this, because dogs are energy recipients.

And you should see this *positive*, because when you focus on being *relaxed* yourself you lead a much happier and healthier life! :-)

Of course, "be relaxed" sounds much easier than it is done - particularly if you have a stressful job (or no job), several small or adolescent kids, problems with your partner, health issues, or a bank account that's so empty that it steals your sleep.

Hence, I feel that dog owners who struggle with dog problems should get the benefit of the doubt and all these potential problem areas in their life be considered. Generally, it is not that dog owners don't *know* any better or don't *want* to improve the dog-human relationship, instead it is all these other **life problems** that make them have 'dog problems'!

(Ah, what splendid diction :-)

Obviously, this book can't address every such area of your life *just* to help you build the best relationship with your dog. Then this book would need 5000 pages or more, and would no longer be a book focusing on **dog training**, but a book on life coaching.

So, all I can do here is to make you aware of the fundamental impact **our state of mind** has on our dog's behavior (and health).

I can't stress this enough:

Our own state of mind <u>fundamentally impacts</u> our dog's behavior and health!

Even when we are just quietly sitting on the couch and we don't *behave* in any way, our state of *mind* <u>will</u> impact on our dog's *behavior*.

I wouldn't go as far as attributing dogs in general telepathic skill, but many dogs certainly have a 'sixth sense'. Many dogs are extremely empathetic. As stressed humans, with no time for anything, many of us may just not notice this (but those probably haven't got the time to come as far as to this page, ha!).

Benevolent

In addition to being <u>relaxed</u>, it is very helpful to be **benevolent** when we train our dog, because I would argue that dogs *feel* how well we mean it with them.

Proof: With certain measures of Dog Care (see later the <u>Care Compendium</u>) and Dog Health (see later the <u>Health Compendium</u>) we need to do things that our dog will not like at all. If a stranger did those things, any dog would outright bite that person!

Vets know this very well. <u>This</u> is why for many examinations they restrain and muzzle or sedate the dog - even when they know that the particular examination doesn't hurt at all! However, when <u>we</u> do those things, our dog will wince but not bite us.

This is so if our dog knows from past experience that we always had in mind to <u>help</u> it. That we never punished or threatened our dog.

Dogs *for sure* have such consciousness, see for example the mentioned book <u>The Intelligence of Dogs: Canine Consciousness and Capabilities</u> (my germanshepherd.org/go/book-intelligence-of-dogs-consciousness).

Confident

I mentioned already that domesticated dogs have a genetically ingrained *quest* to belong to a human Pack. Our modern dogs *need* a human Pack to live and thrive (that's why shelter dogs mentally suffer so quickly - they get very little, if any, interaction in overcrowded shelters).

What I haven't yet mentioned but have explained in more detail in the <u>Puppy Development Guide - Puppy 101</u> is that dogs' genetic heritage also requires them to strive for <u>Pack leadership</u>.

<u>This</u> is why timid dog owners feel dominated by their dog. If we let them, dogs will take over the leadership of our family Pack - whether we have a giant Great Dane or a tiny Chihuahua!

It is these dog owners that complain:

- "My dog always occupies the couch - and even *growls* at me when I try to sit on my couch!"

- "My dog doesn't come when I call her. I have to shout 5 times or hold up a treat before she does one step towards me!"

- "My dog gets really aggressive when all I want is to give him food. But I don't dare to put it in his bowl, he scares me. I don't know what to do!"

If you no longer want to be one of them (or at some point become one of them), you *must* show **confidence**. All dog owners *must* demonstrate confident Pack leadership, each day anew.

Presumably, this is the reason why **Obedience Training** has become so popular (and such a moneymaker): Whoever was the first to write about Dog Obedience Training, did so because (s)he realized that dogs strive for Pack leadership when we let them. All authors that followed copied this idea, and they made their own slight changes to the Obedience Training approach:

- Some focus on physical force

- Others focus on intimidation and raising fear

- Many use electronic gadgets like 'training' collars (do not ever waste your money and dog-human relationship on that!)

- Others disapprove of physical violence but substitute it with shouting

- Some *pull* the dog to whatever it did 'wrong' and 'dip its nose in it'

- Others use sprays (mygermanshepherd.org/go/pepper-spray - this *may* be useful if you cross a loose dog that attacks you, although I'd argue the spray may rather get in your own eyes if you are not careful!)

- Or they use a thunderer whistle (mygermanshepherd.org/go/top-whistle), high-pitched dog whistle (mygermanshepherd.org/go/silent-dog-whistle) or other sounds

- Many lock away their dog - that's why cage-like crates (mygermanshepherd.org/go/metal-cage-crate), ie kennels, have gained otherwise inexplicable popularity!

- And many simply give up on their dog, ie they give the dog to a shelter (or do even worse!)

But *none* of that is necessary! In fact, in recent years we have replaced all these shades of Obedience Training with **Behavior Training** - which is our proprietary dog training approach that underpins our site's Periodicals (free) and my books (not free, no)

Partner

A final, fourth characteristic of the Mindset we need in order to build the best relationship with our dog, I would argue, is that of a 'Partner'.

If not earlier, than at the latest *now* all obedience-focused dog owners, authors, and dog trainers will probably gasp: "Is he nuts? You can't, you *must not* give in to a dog, you must always dominate your dog!".

However, they misunderstand my point. This is not about partnership like between husband and wife, or between close friends. Such dog-human partnership wouldn't even be possible, because:

All equality concepts are human.
For canines, we can only either be subordinate
Pack member or *accepted* Pack leader

Mark the word *accepted* Pack leader. Most dog owners never make it to this level, and many dog trainers never understand the difference. In their dog's view, they are and remain a subordinate Pack member.

116

For the above reason, when I mention 'Partner' I don't mean 'on equal terms'. This would be devastating in a dog-human relationship.

Instead, with 'Partner' mindset I mean the opposite of a 'Master-Servant' mindset - because that is what we must <u>not</u> practice if we want to train our dog in a way to build the best relationship. I haven't yet come up with a better word than 'Partner', hence I use that.

If in our mindset our dog is a 'Partner', then we seed a <u>great relationship</u>. Conversely, if in our mindset we are the master of our dog that is the servant that executes our never-ending plethora of commands, then we seed <u>oppression</u>.

Now some may be thinking: "What's the problem with oppression? It's an ANIMAL for God's sake!"

Well, I am telling you right now and here what's the problem with oppression, and what's the problem with the ever so popular **Obedience Training**:

In case of oppression through excessive use of commands (or worse!) - like with Obedience Training - because of the dog's inherited quest to strive for Pack leadership, we *condition* our dog to do just that, all the time, to counter the oppression!

That is the *opposite* of <u>Desensitization</u> (p~224). So, not smart at all.

<u>This</u> is why so many dog owners are not getting anywhere with their dog training: They shout "STOP IT" multiple times but their dog keeps on barking anyway, they insist "COME HERE" multiple times but their dog doesn't come anyway, ... etc.

Instead, with the Partner mindset, we will command our dog <u>less</u>, and motivate our dog <u>more</u>. Thus our dog will feel *less* desire to demonstrate its leadership in our family Pack. We condition our dog *away* from that. We *desensitize* our dog from this genetic quest!

So frankly: It is smart to have a **Partner mindset**.

Now, don't get me wrong, I admit that some dog breeds and crosses are more approachable to training with **this mindset** than others. And some dogs of the *same* breed are easier to train than others.

However, for the very reason just mentioned I would argue that *regardless* of breed and cross, it is *always* better to apply the **Partner mindset** to dog training than to apply the Master-Servant mindset.

Only the emphasis between the use of commands and of motivation I would vary, subject to the success I see with the individual dog. Having say the generally very dominant Bull Terrier, Pitbull, Rottweiler, or Chihuahua does <u>not</u> exclude these dogs from this training mindset.

In fact, it seems much harder for us humans to make the transition from Master-Servant mindset to **Partner mindset** than it is for the *most dominant* canines to become receptible to training based on the Partner mindset!

If you doubt your dog's suitability for this training approach, then why not give your own mindset a try? ;-)

Try to transition to the Partner mindset

You can't lose anything. It won't make your dog more aggressive, and it won't worsen your dog-human relationship.

Reward Tools

There exist 5 Types of Rewards, and when we want to use Rewards as a training tool we must know when to use which.

Praise

Praise is an excellent reward for a dog, and we have already discussed this in the context of Energy Tools (p~39) under **Stimulants** (see Praise, p~91).

But note that we should only use **Praise** when we feel we can control our voice, because for Praise we solely use our voice - and obviously we should never use a training tool that we cannot control.

In other words, if you fear you might shriek, yell, or whatever, then *don't* use Praise as a reward, instead use Affection or the other Reward Tools.

Affection

Various forms of <u>Affection</u> we have already discussed in the context of **Energy Tools**: <u>Chin Stroking</u> (p~58), <u>Chest Stroking</u> (p~60), <u>Belly Stroking</u> (p~61), <u>Back Stroking</u> (p~83), and <u>Head Stroking</u> (p~85).

Cuddle I haven't put in there solely because cuddle can mean so many different forms of affection: snuggling, hugging, embracing,...?

Hugging and embracing certainly are <u>Stimulants</u> though. Also, it is unlikely that our dog experiences them as a **Reward**. Rather, dogs find them annoying, but bear them because they notice that <u>we</u> fancy them.

In my experience, all forms of **Affection** can be used as Reward Tools - *except* hugging/embracing our dog into a headlock. Just like we typically don't like to be headlocked ourselves, dogs certainly don't like this either. It is <u>not</u> considered a Reward.

The fact that our dog may bear it, doesn't mean (s)he likes it. I would bet that *no* healthy dog likes to be embraced. This form of affection is against canine nature. If dogs bury their head into something (they sometimes do), that's voluntary. But if we bury our dog's head between our chest and arms, that's not voluntary.

It's not that we cannot do this, we *can* (if we have developed a trusting relationship with our dog). But the point is, it is <u>not</u> felt as a **Reward**. Remember that it doesn't matter how much *we* believe that something is a Reward, if our dog doesn't like it then it is no Reward.

The training implication? Well, <u>motivation</u> (the core of our Behavior Training) - and equally 'positive reinforcement' (today's core of Obedience Training) - obviously cannot work if our dog doesn't find it *positive* what we do to reward the dog!

Also, with your own dog, you hopefully know what (s)he likes and what (s)he *tolerates*, but using **Affection** with another person's dog can be outright dangerous: Particularly patting on the head and embracing require some bonding time before they can be considered safe.

This is why children often get bitten when they meet a dog on the street and all they want is to show their affection.

Even with your own dog, the next time when you feel like patting your dog's head or throwing your arms around your dog's neck and taking your dog in a headlock, think about whether you would like that yourself?

The fact that our dog tolerates something doesn't necessarily mean that our dog likes it!

To keep your children safe, ideally teach them: "Do what dogs like, not what you like". Then your children will likely ask: "What do dogs like?" - And you can reply: "Look at the dog's body language to find out". And then you'll probably need to show your children some examples - best would be photographic examples, like with the mentioned photographic guide to canine body language (mygermanshepherd.org/go/canine-body-language).

I haven't actually *asked* dogs, but from diligent observation I would argue that from all forms of

Affection <u>Chin Stroking</u> (p~58), <u>Chest Stroking</u> (p~60), and <u>Belly Stroking</u> (p~61) are most dogs' favorites.

Note that all of these are <u>Sedatives</u> (p~45)! Indeed, if they can choose, dogs *want* to stay calm.

I hear you screaming: "But not my dog!"

Yes, you are right, there are probably a few dogs that are *so* different, *so* special, that they may *enjoy* to be headlocked, ha! ;-)

Anyway, if you choose either of *these* types of **Affection**, it's likely that your dog truly feels **rewarded**. And that's the key to motivate your dog to repeat a certain behavior that you like to see.

Toys & Play

Toys and Play both are also Energy Tools (namely Stimulants, p~78). With Toys and Play we *raise* our dog's energy level, ie we want our dog to be more active.

Thus, in situations where we rather want our dog to calm down, we will not use Toys and Play as the **Reward**. Or at least we will then give a Chew Toy which raises the energy level *least* (see my note at the end of Toys, p~109).

Makes all more sense already, right?

Good :-)

Play

As a <u>Reward</u> (p~126), we consider <u>Play</u> as <u>Together-time</u> with our dog, ie we spend time *with* our dog, not merely observing our dog for safety reasons.

During playtime we may use a <u>Toy</u>, or we may play without involving a toy (like say when we play hide-and-seek, or we do competitive sprints, or we go swimming with our dog).

Toys

Conversely, when we reward our dog with a <u>Toy</u>, then this typically is not Together-time. Nonetheless, what many dog owners don't do, we must <u>casually observe</u> our dog for safety reasons because almost all Toys can disintegrate, or even be swallowed entirely if they are small from the outset.

Exception: The <u>Varsity Ball</u> (mygermanshepherd. org/go/varsity-ball). 100% indestructible, and too large to be swallowed. So, *after* initial observation (to gauge our dog's play-drive) we can indeed let the dog play alone with this one. The Varsity Ball is the only autonomous dog exercise instrument I know of. But it certainly is *not* suitable for small dogs, weak dogs, and old dogs.

Apart from the casual observation, when we give our dog a **Toy** we expect the dog to play alone with it. - As with so many things, there is of course an exception (Puzzle Toys).

Since dogs' preferences are different (even among the same breed) and each dog's preferences change over time (but not as often as human preferences change!), Toys in the six Toy Categories (p~97) also **reward** each dog in different ways.

However, even when you get a new dog, in no time you will find out which Toy Categories (and which Toys in these) seem to reward your dog best.

Therefore, having one or two Toys of *each* Toy Category is much better than getting plenty of Toys but unknowingly just from within two or three Toy Categories. This now also explained why we discussed Toy Categories above (p~97).

Real-Life Treats

I can't remember to have seen a single dog book that doesn't make the claim that dogs have only a *very* short-term memory. That's why you shall "punish your dog immediately" say for urinating in the house (no, you really shouldn't punish your dog at all!), and that's why you shall "reward your dog immediately" say for sitting down when you commanded SIT.

But no, fact is that canines have a much better long-term memory than most humans can imagine or want to admit. This is why **Real-Life Treats** really are considered a **Reward** by our dog.

What are Real-Life Treats?

"Real-Life Treats are any action that dogs feel as an improvement to their often very monotonous dog life".

Right! :-)

As long as our dog can still make the connection between the Real-Life Treat and its own earlier behavior, the dog will understand that it is a Reward.

Examples of Real-Life Treats

- Going on an immediate off-leash or loose-leash walk (p~65)

- Unrestricted going through the door

- Providing comfy Resting Places near us (p~66)

- Taking off the Short Leash (p~86)

- Swapping Short Leash for Long Line (p~64)

- Taking off the Collar (only if at home!)

- Spending Together-time (p~125)

- Swimming (if liked)

- Going to the beach

- Providing tasty Dog Meals (p~168)

- etc

The key is: In order to have **Real-Life Treats** being experienced by our dog as a Reward, we may need to help our dog to make the connection between

Treat and earlier behavior. This should become clearer with the following usage examples.

Examples How to Use Real-Life Treats

1) Going on an immediate walk

Say our dog nudged us earlier to go for a walk but we've been busy and signaled our dog to go away so that we can concentrate on our work a bit longer.

Now our dog nudges us again and we look on our watch and realize that an hour has passed!

We demonstratively look again on our watch and then at our dog and with excitement say something like: "Oh, you've been so quiet for an HOUR? Let's go for a WALK right now!" - and we get up and go for a walk straight away!

Now most if not all dogs will *connect* the immediate walk with having been quiet for what seemed like forever to the dog. In other words: Dogs do understand that the immediate walk is a **Reward**.

Note that our entire behavior, including the demonstrative look on the watch, helps our dog to build that connection.

After a few times our dog will know: "If I keep quiet for what seems to me like forever, my Pack member/leader looks at this thing on his/her arm, and if this thing signals 'okay' then I am rewarded with an immediate walk."

2) Unrestricted going through the door

Normally, when we go for a walk with our dog we should always be the first to go through the front door, because that's what dogs expect the Pack leader to do. Actually, we would follow a certain routine before we go for the walk (for more see the Leash Training guide: mygermanshepherd.org/go/ leash-training-guide).

Now say during this routine our dog heeled well and did not pull towards the door. Our dog demonstrated that (s)he knows that such behavior would only further delay the walk.

This is another opportunity for a Real Life Treat: When we are pleased with our dog's behavior inside the house before we go for a walk, then why not show our dog that we are pleased, and reward our dog with canceling the rest of our standard routine?

So this time, we open the door wide straight away, step aside and let our dog get through the door first (subject to this being safe, no high-traffic road in front).

Again, now most if not all dogs will *connect* the unrestricted going through the door (without our prior standard routine, which the dog remembers very well!) with having matched our SSCD movements inside the house well.

In other words: Dogs do understand that cutting short our normally lengthier routine and letting our dog freely through the front door first is a **Reward**.

3) Resting Places near us

Most dog owners (and trainers!) are unaware how important it is that our dog has its dedicated Resting Place near us (p~66) in *every* room where we want (or allow) our dog to be with us. As explained earlier, this is a crucial everyday Sedative to make our dog relaxed and balanced.

Now say, you don't want your dog to be next to your feet in the kitchen and begging for food all the time. But say, today you don't want to exclude your dog from the kitchen either because you are going to be in the kitchen for what seems like all day (some people are).

So you left the kitchen door open (if it has one at all) and your dog kept well out of the kitchen nonetheless (p~68). But your kitchen is large, and by remaining in front of the kitchen entrance your dog can't be as close to you as (s)he would normally be.

Now you *could* put a blanket in a safe corner of the kitchen and allow your dog to lie down on it (*inside* the kitchen, although you normally don't allow that). You provide a Resting Place near you (for as long as your dog complies and is lying down on the blanket).

Your dog would experience this as a **Reward**, because (s)he makes the connection between having stayed out of the kitchen when you said so, and now being allowed *in* the kitchen if (s)he remains on the blanket.

I hope these three examples gave you an idea how you can use <u>Real-Life Treats</u> as a Reward for your dog.

Unless your dog's mental capabilities have never been nurtured much (maybe rescue dog?), I bet that (s)he *does* make the necessary connection between behavior and reward! - And if you think your dog won't, then I'd strongly suggest you look at the great book <u>Brain Games for Dogs</u> (mygermanshepherd. org/go/book-brain-games-for-dogs).

Food Treats

Every dog owner knows how to use <u>Food Treats</u> as a Reward, so I guess we don't need to discuss this. ;-)

Nonetheless, a few notes on **Food Treats** seem helpful, just in case:

- IF you use Food Treats, then they should always be more tempting than the regular <u>Dog Meal</u> (p~161), or else for example your <u>Recall</u> will not work reliably

- Food Treats should not be given in the hour before or after a Dog Meal (or else it disturbs the <u>Feeding Routine</u>, p~138)

- Food Treats <u>must not</u> be given right before or after heavy exercise, or else the food may be thrown back up and suffocate the dog, or it may lead to <u>Bloat</u> (see later the <u>Health Compendium</u>)

- Food Treats should *not* be thrown on the ground or in the crate, but <u>given from our hand</u> (to practice <u>Bite Inhibition</u> (p~72), and to discourage from Scavenging)

135

- Dry Food Treats *require* that our dog has immediate free access to a water bowl (mygerm anshepherd.org/go/spill-proof-dog-travel-bowl) - or else the food can get stuck in the esophagus and suffocate the dog or may lead to Bloat, as just mentioned

- Food Treats are not necessary at all! While it is okay to give the occasional Food Treat (unless you fear Obesity), be aware that **treat training** your dog has negative behavior implications! More on this will be in the Training Compendium.

- When you want to give Food Treats, try to limit it to healthy treats like these: mygermanshep herd.org/

Food Tools

The term 'Food Tools' may sound strange but it just means that we will use matters revolving around **food** as a Tool for our dog training approach.

This is the smartest thing we can do, since the prime quest of dogs is to secure food (see <u>Lip Licking</u>, p~79). Hence **Food Tools** typically give the best immediate dog training success in a given situation and environment (but in a *different* situation or environment dogs then often need to be <u>re-trained</u>, see p~89).

While probably all dog owners know this bit, what they don't realize is that they are not confined to using <u>Food Treats</u> for their dog training. No, dog owners indeed have a much broader (and better!) repertoire at their disposal. See all chapters below.

The most important **Food Tool** is the <u>Feeding Routine</u> (next chapter), which is a clear-cut process *how* to serve food to our dog for maximum training benefit (and to avoid practically all dog behavior problems)!

Other **Food Tools** are the type of <u>Dog Meals</u> we serve our dog (p~161), <u>Consistent Meal Times</u> (p~162), <u>Treat Toys</u> (p~94) and <u>Food Treats</u> (p~134).

———————————

Again, you see that **Dog Training Tools** can of course belong to *several* Toolsets. But to know to *which* they belong is helpful so as to use them <u>right</u>.

This now also explained why I provided the <u>Dog Training Toolkit Mindmap</u> further above (p~34).

Using the Dog Training Tools <u>right</u> is then **a matter of practice** - which I can't help you with because I am not your neighbor. ;-)

———————————

Feeding Routine

The **Feeding Routine** is not only the best
Food Tool, it is the overall
BEST Dog Training Tool of all!

The Feeding Routine comprises:

- Gesture-Eating (p~141)

- Making our dog SIT before eating (p~147)

- Deferring the Meal (p~149)

- Canceling the Meal (p~150)

- Disturbing the Meal (an *exception*, p~152)

- Serving the Meal in an Eat-Slow bowl (p~155)

- Immediately Taking Away Leftovers (p~157)

- and various points revolving around all of this

Why the Feeding Routine is the most powerful Dog Training Tool of all

The Feeding Routine is so immensely powerful because *food* determines the survival of the dog. A dog doesn't really know if - and when - (s)he will get another meal, *unless* Consistent Meal Times (p~162) and our overall behavior have established a certain *expectation* of our dog which (s)he learned (s)he can rely on.

Thus any Food Tool we use has a special meaning to our dog, and it will influence our dog's behavior.

The **Feeding Routine** has the biggest impact because:

- The Feeding Routine is the most powerful Tool to establish ourselves (and *every* family member!) as *accepted* Pack leader

- The Feeding Routine offers a much better chance to demonstrate Consistency (p~75) than say handing out a Treat Toy (p~94) or a Food Treat (p~134)

- Consistency is what trains a dog best. Canines thrive on *routine* behavior.

For example, we can throw a ball 20 times - and our dog will fetch it everytime like it was the first time. Or we always pick up the car keys before we leave - and the key sound alone may make our dog speed towards us, although (s)he knows (s)he won't come with us.

Indeed, if we perform the whole Feeding Routine consistently the same way, our dog will soon act exactly as we want (and not only during meal times, ha!) - often without us having to give *any* command at all.

If this reminds you of my earlier brief introduction to our **Behavior Training** approach (where I said we will use far less commands than are required with **Obedience Training**), then you hit home!

Indeed, our Feeding Routine is a core component of our Behavior Training - it is the second-most important component, after our own Mindset that we need for Behavior Training.

So let's look at the elements of our Feeding Routine:

Gesture-Eating

Like **Obedience Training** can only be successful if you use some form of force, fear, or bribe - **Behavior Training** can only be successful if we ourselves behave in a certain way (*without* using any force, fear, or bribe)!

One such behavior required from us is that we make a performance of **Gesture-Eating** before we serve our dog a meal.

'Performance' - yes, this word says it already: It will be most FUN for us and most effective for our dog when we imagine that we are the actor in a theater play. :-)

So, do make sure that you fully understand (and ideally apply!) this Tool. Once you perform Gesture-Eating consistently over say a week, you will notice so dramatic (positive!) behavior changes of your dog that you will regret you haven't used this Tool earlier.

We shouldn't give guarantees as a book author, but here I say without hesitation: Guaranteed!

Most likely, the positive behavior changes will already become noticeable after the first two or three times of Gesture-Eating.

However, here I slightly disagree with Doggy Dan Abdelnoor (mygermanshepherd.org/go/online-dog-trainer) who believes we should make a performance of Gesture-Eating before *every* meal, for the entire life of our dog. In my experience this is normally not necessary. It seems sufficient to do the following:

Until the end of **Family Socialization** (about age 3 months, if we got our dog as a puppy), we better perform Gesture-Eating before every meal, with as few exceptions as possible because this early stage of puppyhood *conditions* a dog's later behavior to an exceptional extent (for more see the Puppy Development Guide - Puppy 101: mygermanshepherd.org/go/puppy-development-guide).

Similarly, if we get an adult dog from a shelter or a prior owner, the first four to six weeks are crucial to show our new dog that we are the Pack leader (who in the wild too always eats first).

Why the first four to six weeks? Because, when subjected to a new environment, the dog's neurons establish new connections (called *facilitation*). It is these new neuronal connections that shape the behavior of our dog going forward!

So I would strongly recommend to (ideally) gesture-eat before every meal during this period. Thereafter, it seems okay to perform Gesture-Eating less frequently - the older the dog gets, the less - *unless* we have reason to complain about our dog's behavior.

And with a **Senior Dog** it typically is not necessary to perform Gesture-Eating at all.

How to perform Gesture-Eating

- We symbolically (or literally if we like the taste) eat a bit of our dog's meal from its bowl, so to say spooning it into our mouth (pretending it)

- The more 'dog problems' we are facing, the *longer* we should perform Gesture-Eating. Likewise, if we just newly got an adult dog (from the shelter or from a prior owner), a *longer* Gesture-Eating performance seems advisable (one to two minutes!)

- Then we ask our dog to sit down a bit further back (*during* Gesture-Eating we should only ask our dog to SIT if we are scared that say our new dog might jump at us to get the food)

- Only if our dog calmly sits (say two meters away from us), *then* we place down the bowl - either already filled with food, or we fill it now

- If our (new) dog still shows the slightest form of food aggression, we should <u>not</u> fill the food bowl before placing it down; instead we better fill it on the ground *very slowly* while observing the subsequent points

- <u>Because</u> we don't want our dog to storm towards the food bowl immediately, instead we want to be able to safely and calmly fill the bowl before our dog even approaches it

- Thus we require our dog to remain in SIT position until we give the <u>signal</u> to go to its bowl and eat: "<u>COME</u> (p~184), enjoy your meal", or "Dinner is ready", or "Eat, my darling", or an inviting <u>Hand Cue</u> (p~175), or whatever you fancy :-)

- Only now our dog eats - and we will <u>not disturb</u> our dog during its meal (apart from the subsequent exception)

Note that we *only* put down our dog's bowl when (s)he is sitting calm, not as long as (s)he is standing, wagging its tail, whining or barking!

Who to involve in Gesture-Eating

Every family member must be involved in Gesture-Eating. This is crucially important.

Even when we have a small baby, we will use a <u>baby sling</u> (mygermanshepherd.org/go/baby-sling) and have our baby right in front of us when we perform Gesture-Eating! This will show our dog that our baby is its Pack leader too. *Every* child in the family must take part in the Gesture-Eating ritual, at least once a day.

It is those dog owners where this *doesn't* happen that hit the news with headlines like "7-year old boy bitten by family dog" (and of course those that don't employ Gesture-Eating at all).

To safeguard even the smallest family members, *everyone* must be involved in Gesture-Eating.

Sit to Eat

As mentioned, <u>sitting before eating</u> is part of the Gesture-Eating ritual, but even at times when we *don't* want to gesture-eat before our dog, we should always make our dog SIT before (s)he gets a meal.

Ideally even before getting a <u>Food Treat</u> (p~134), but *not* when outside and in winter - unless you want your dog to get a bladder infection, like so many dog owners seem to be keen on: They make their dog sit at every street corner. :-(

Sitting before eating (for 10 seconds up to a minute, if you have the time) has a substantial **calming effect** on our domesticated dogs. Sitting is not a natural position for dogs (wild dogs hardly ever sit, they either stand or lie down). Sitting is not relaxing for dogs, but it *does* calm them down nonetheless.

When calm, dogs eat much slower - which is so much healthier: Gulping down the food can rapidly lead to Bloat (which for dogs can be a life-threatening condition!), Vomiting, Diarrhea, and Regurgitating (which brings digestive enzymes back up and results in that familiar 'bad breath' of so many dogs). For all see later the <u>Health Compendium</u>.

In addition to the health benefits, **Sitting before eating** also has significant <u>behavior benefits</u>:

- Sitting before eating manifests our *acceptance* as Pack leader

- Sitting before eating reduces the chance of Food Aggression and Territorial Aggression

- Sitting before eating reduces the chance of Scavenging when there is an opportunity.

And of course, **Sitting before eating** gives us safety and peace while we are filling the food bowl: Little is more annoying than a dog that has its head already half-buried in the place where we try to put the dog food - in the <u>food bowl</u> (p~155)!

Deferring the Meal

When our dog is not calm during our <u>Gesture Eating</u> (p~141), we simply **Defer the meal**.

We put it back and do whatever we want to do. Then, after 5, 10, or 15 minutes, we come back and make another attempt. A maximum of three attempts for adult dogs seems sensible (we make only two attempts).

The added beauty of deferring the meal is: It will demonstrate our Pack leadership <u>whether or not</u> we subsequently have to <u>Cancel the Meal</u>.

Canceling the Meal

There are two situations for <u>Canceling a Dog Meal</u>:

- If upon the third attempt of <u>Gesture Eating</u> (p~141) our dog is still not calm

- If our dog <u>walks away from food</u> (p~157)

Canceling a meal means we serve no food until the next scheduled meal time.

Do *not* worry, it is not a problem if a dog doesn't get a meal (dogs can survive three days without food) - but it is a severe problem if a dog doesn't get sufficient drinking water!

If our dog is on two meals a day (which should be the absolute minimum to stay healthy and well-behaved!), then **Canceling the meal** is a no-brainer.

If your dog is on only one meal a day, then I urge you to change that immediately to two meals a day (obviously splitting the amount of food in half).

Dogs that get three meals a day, won't even feel really hungry if they don't get one of these meals: A healthy dog's digestive process takes about 8 hours (while our own takes up to about 20 hours because we not only *digest* but also *ferment* food - which takes longest).

What **Canceling the meal** will do is, it will demonstrate to our dog that <u>we</u> are the Pack leader - who decides over the <u>Feeding Routine</u> - like in the wild, as well as during **Litter Socialization** of our domesticated dogs (as explained in the <u>Puppy Development Guide - Puppy 101</u>).

When puppies or adult dogs don't comply, they are barred from the food. Yes indeed, in a dog pack they learn very quickly to comply with the Pack leader's <u>Feeding Routine</u> (p~138) - and so it should be with us as well.

Disturbing the Meal - the Exception when it is okay

For most dog owners, and particularly for our children, it is best to remember the simple rule "Never disturb a dog's meal".

Despite this rule, there is an exception:

- When we have a puppy, and

- When we newly got an adult dog from the shelter or from a prior owner.

In these cases it should help more than it harms to make an exception to the rule "Never disturb a dog's meal". In all other circumstances the remaining Bite Inhibition training opportunities (p~73) should suffice.

In these two cases, once a while we may decide to ask our dog to STOP eating, step back and SIT down. When our dog complies, we add some *very tasty* morsel to the bowl, and then we give the signal to continue eating.

Benefits:

- This helps to prevent that our dog develops or continues Food Aggression (and potentially other forms of aggression too)

- It strengthens our position as Pack leader

- It trains <u>Bite Inhibition</u> (p~72)

- It will make our dog understand that when we want it to stop eating, something even greater is going to happen (immediate learning), and we have our dog's best interest at heart (long-term learning, canine consciousness)

- It helps to prevent Scavenging, because our dog learns to eat only when we signal it.

Drawbacks:

- When you do this too often, too long or too pathetic, it <u>badgers</u> the dog - which is *bad* for developing a great relationship

- Even such 'positive' meal interruption (getting an extra *very tasty* morsel) creates <u>stress</u> - which is *bad* for a dog, particularly during meal times.

So, I wouldn't do this more than once per meal, not every meal, and *without* making a performance out of this.

Instead, just a quick gentle interruption with as minimal disturbance as possible, maybe once a week.

Unless our dog shows signs of *any* form of aggression - in this case I would temporarily do this twice or thrice weekly (but not more, to avoid that the dog can build an *expectation* of the interruption, in which case it wouldn't be as helpful).

Eat-Slow Bowl

Using an Eat-Slow bowl also is another scene of the same theater set: The best of these dog bowls really slow down the food intake substantially - being the natural extension of our Gesture Eating (p~141) performance, which too is a demonstration of *tranquility*.

In my experience and based on the feedback of thousands of dog owners, this Eat-Slow bowl (my germanshepherd.org/go/eat-slow-bowl) is the best:

- good for short and long tongue

- pretty much skid-free

- slows down food intake without badgering the dog (many Eat-Slow bowls do upset the dog!)

BUT: a) it's made of polypropylene (so not exactly great to eat from *every day*), and b) it's fairly expensive (particularly when you consider it's made of 'plastic').

The second-best Eat-Slow bowl (mygermanshephe rd.org/go/eat-slow-bowl-metal) is much cheaper *and* it's made of stainless steel. But this one is not suitable for small dogs with short tongue. In that case the <u>third-best bowl</u> (mygermanshepherd.org/ go/eat-slow-bowl-third-best) is better.

Important is to choose a bowl that is skid-free and won't badger our dog. Because there's no point in stressing out the dog when (s)he eats, pushing the bowl all over the place and making a mess everywhere (which then stresses out ourselves too, ha!).

Remember: The purpose of an **Eat-Slow bowl** is to **reduce stress**, not to increase stress. Because, for canines much more than for humans (but less than for pigs), **stress** results in health and behavior problems!

Taking Away Leftovers

A final component of our Feeding Routine (p~138) is to immediately take away any food our dog leaves behind.

Meaning, when our dog doesn't finish its Meal (p~161) or doesn't seek a Food Treat we provide (p~134), we instantly take away the food and cancel that meal/treat. (S)he won't get it anymore. See Canceling the Meal (p~150).

Like in the wild, food left behind is gone! Our dog will quickly learn to finish a Meal and eat the offered Treat - instead of trying to demonstrate its Pack leadership.

Why? Because, if we are not consistent here, dogs quickly use any FOOD situation to effectively (re-) establish their Pack leader position (remember, food is their key trigger).

To the untrained dog owner's eyes it may not appear as such, but by walking away from food, most of the time dogs try to win the upper hand in the Pack.

By walking away from food dogs are communicating:

"Look, it is *me* who controls the food. I can eat when I want. You can spoon that food into my bowl whenever and however you like, nonetheless I will tell *you* when I want to eat!"

Only by **Taking Away Leftovers** immediately, we can successfully establish ourselves as Pack leader (who controls the food). The whole Gesture Eating (p~141) performance would be pointless if we didn't also take away any leftovers.

Caveat

If our dog's behavior suggests that (s)he really doesn't *want* to eat what we are serving, then by all means we <u>won't</u> force our dog (like in "you don't get anything else").

Because many dogs *do* know if they cannot digest a certain food. They feel pain, they may suffer from Bloat, Vomiting, Constipation, or Diarrhea (which indeed is a symptom of constipation too, see the incredibly helpful book of <u>Dr Wes Jones: Cure Constipation Now</u>: mygermanshepherd.org/go/book-cure-constipation-now).

Particularly when we adopt an adult dog from a prior owner or from a shelter (p~27), we just *cannot* know our new dog's <u>food intolerances</u> (see later the <u>Care Compendium</u>) or even <u>food allergies</u> (see later the <u>Health Compendium</u>).

In any case, I would never 'force' a dog to eat a particular food, even less so if I were to feed some cheap processed dog food with loads of unspecified ingredients and additives (which I don't).

Anyway, this caveat rarely affects the Dog Training Tool <u>Taking Away Leftovers</u>: If our dog's behavior signals that by all means (s)he doesn't *want* to eat certain food, then this normally becomes already apparent when we fill the bowl.

160

In such case I would look the dog in the eyes and if I see any sign of sadness I know I better get some different food (and quality food).

A dog's "turning away from food to demonstrate Pack leadership" does not involve sadness in the eyes, instead the dog will demonstratively <u>walk away</u> from the food.

Dog Meals

The topic of <u>Dog Meals</u> has minor relevance for our subject here, **Dog Training**, but major relevance for the subject of Dog Care. Therefore I will primarily discuss it in the <u>Care Compendium</u>.

However, in terms of Dog Training, the reason why **Dog Meals** *can* be used as a Training Tool is that dogs obviously notice the difference between say the ordinary every-day kibble serving and the special-day homemade gourmet lunch. :-)

So, a tasty Dog Meal indeed is a <u>Food Tool</u> (p~136) as well as a <u>Reward Tool</u> (see <u>Real-Life Treats</u>, p~127).

In addition, **Dog Meals** are a Training Tool in terms of **House Training**: Only when we serve Dog Meals that avoid Vomiting and Diarrhea, we get a dog that can be left alone in the house (and with free run of the house!) without making a mess. For more see the House Training guide (mygermanshepherd. org/go/house-training-guide).

Consistent Meal Times

Consistent Meal Times a Dog Training Tool??

Oh yes! **Consistent Meal Times** is a Dog Training Tool because:

- Only the continuous experience of Consistent Meal Times can help our dog to <u>desensitize</u> (p~217) from the canine quest to grab every food opportunity like it could be the last!

- Thus Consistent Meal Times also drastically <u>reduce Scavenging</u> during dog walking (particularly when off-leash)

- Likewise, Consistent Meal Times drastically reduce sneaking the turkey, cookies, or even that dump chunk of butter from the table (a study found that dogs routinely do 'kitchen counter surfing' when Pack members aren't around :-)

- Further, Consistent Meal Times reduce <u>Coprophagy</u> (although eating feces is *not* out of pure hunger)

- Consistent Meal Times help our dog to *relax* because the metabolism adapts to the Meal Times, which prevents the early signal 'hungry!' - this is crucially important because a <u>relaxed dog</u> is a much more well-behaved dog!

- In addition, Consistent Meal Times help ourselves enormously because we can <u>plan dedicated training sessions</u> for the times when quick training success is most likely (the two hours before each meal)

- Likewise, Consistent Meal Times help our dog to focus on our training (and to comply with our <u>Commands</u> (p~184) where we use them), instead of focusing on the next-best opportunity to get some food (meal or treat)

- Finally, only Consistent Meal Times allow us to <u>renounce 'treat training'</u> without feeling bad about it!

There are *tons* of dog trainers out there who teach dog owners explicitly or visually to use loads of <u>Food Treats</u> (I call that **treat training**). Basically all dog trainers who try to renounce force and fear in their training approach (good!), but don't know how to <u>treat</u> their dog (let alone <u>motivate</u> their dog) without Food Treats (sad).

In addition to all the above benefits for our **Dog Training**, <u>Consistent Meal Times</u> of course also have **health benefits** (see later in the <u>Health Compendium</u>).

Treat Toys

Treat Toys are those small dog toys where we put an even smaller treat inside for our dog to discover, see Treat Toys (p~96). The best Treat Toys are those that are also Puzzle Toys (p~97), because these train our dog's mental capabilities, and thus prevent boredom much better.

> Boredom in dogs is the **PRIME** reason for what we experience as 'dog problems'!

Since we place **food** inside, all the principles revolving around food that we have already discussed apply to **Treat Toys** too, in particular:

- We shouldn't throw the Treat Toy on the ground or in the crate, but rather invite our dog to COME (p~184) and collect it - remember, positives: let dog come to us; negatives or neutral: we walk to our dog!

Food Tools

- If our dog <u>doesn't come</u> (doesn't want the food in the toy), we keep the toy and put it away - *without* saying anything, looking at our dog, or touching our dog (show no grudge/ disappointment)

- When our dog <u>stops trying</u> to retrieve the food in the toy (leaves the toy alone), we also take the toy away (again, without grudge)

- We deduct all *amounts* of hidden foods from the upcoming meal - meaning the hidden foods (like all <u>Food Treats</u>, p~134) can be very different to <u>Dog Meals</u> (indeed Food Treats should always be more tempting), but we avoid making our dog obese by deducting treat *amounts* from meals.

Other than this, we can refill the <u>Treat Toy</u> once or twice, but we should *not* leave a Treat Toy (or indeed any Toy) with our dog for several hours - like most dog owners do.

Why?

167

- Again, this would give our dog the impression that (s)he can <u>control possessions</u>, which would undermine our effort to become the *accepted* Pack leader

- Having the same Toy or Toys *available* for hours on end <u>accelerates boredom</u>

- This is true even with a *choice* between multiple Toys - which also makes it harder for us to notice when <u>Toys disintegrate</u> (and thus parts may be swallowed!)

- <u>A bored dog destroys Toys</u> - See for yourself: When you frequently swap the Toys, they last much longer (because your dog values them more, is less bored, and thus less destructive)

Whenever we need to occupy our dog with a <u>Toy</u> (p~94) - because we are too busy to <u>play</u> with our dog (p~100) - we should by all means at least **take a small break** to <u>swap the Toy</u> every hour or so (and maybe to consider a walk with the dog).

In addition, this gives us plenty more opportunities for <u>Bite Inhibition</u> training (p~72), as of course we swap toys from the mouth (but let <u>the dog</u> take initiative, don't shove a toy in the dog's mouth).

For the same reasons as mentioned above I would suggest to <u>even swap a Chew Toy</u> against another <u>Chew Toy</u> (p~94) after an hour (max).

With a **Treat Toy** it's probably better to swap it against another Toy which is *not* a Treat Toy after an hour (max). But with Treat Toys I like to watch anyway - how fast the dog discovers the treat. :-)

When you have kids in the house (or you are young at heart), **Treat Toys** and particularly <u>Puzzle Toys</u> (p~98) offer amazing scope for <u>Playing games</u> (p~100). When you have two dogs (maybe inviting a neighbor's dog), even more so. You'll have loads of FUN with your dog!

Food Treats

There was already a good list of advice on Food Treats under Reward Tools (p~119).

Attention Tools

On to the penultimate Toolset - Attention Tools!

As the name suggests, **Attention Tools** are Dog Training Tools that we can use to raise our dog's attention (concentration, focus).

Most of the time, we want to get our dog to concentrate on *us* (this is easiest), but sometimes we may want to direct our dog's attention on an object, or even on another person.

Note that some **Attention Tools** are also Energy Tools (p~39), and both Toolsets impact on our dog's mindset or mental state (p~100).

However, the key differences between the two:

- Attention either is there or it isn't, while the energy state is a scale of increasing intensity (the term energy level makes this clearer)

- Attention is mood-neutral - if there's any mood involved, it's due to our dog's energy state

- It's much easier for a dog (and for us!) to lose attention than to lose a high energy level!

- Attention Tools have a success-or-failure result, while Energy Tools can be fine-tuned for success

Further differences between the two will become clearer as we progress.

Using Body Language

Adding Body Language to Attention Tools may seem a bit odd: We are (unconsciously) expressing ourselves through body movements all the time, and depending on the type of movement it can in addition be a Sedative (p~45), a Stimulant (p~76), a Distraction Tool (p~193), or even a Reward Tool (namely when we show Affection, p~120).

Nonetheless it fits here best because:

- Dogs focus much more on our body language than what we say - they give our body language more **Attention**

- The tool is *Using* **Body Language**, and when we consciously *use* our body as a Dog Training Tool, then we will indeed foremost draw our dog's **Attention** - *before* (maybe) the calming, stimulating, distracting, or rewarding effect is felt.

This book certainly cannot go into detail on using our body language (that would require a book on its own!). But a great guide on human body language *in general* comes from Allan Pease (mygermanshepherd.

org/go/human-body-language). Should I ever find the time, I'd love to publish a guide on human body language towards dogs, because that seems not to exist yet, and I know it would help dog owners immensely.

So let me only draw your attention (ha!) to two simple aspects of using our body language as a **Dog Training Tool** to raise our dog's **Attention**:

- Arm Movements, and

- Hand Cues

First example: Arm Movements

You will know that when you move your arm, your dog is (briefly) concentrating on you. An Arm Movement raises your dog's attention.

However, we can move our arm in different ways: slow or fast, and towards or away from our body.

Have you noticed that this impacts on your dog's concentration on you?

You may have noticed that when you make a *fast* arm movement, your dog does concentrate on you, but only very briefly. While when you make a *slow* arm movement, your dog should be concentrating on you much longer - even after your arm movement finished. Did you notice this?

The slower we move our arm, the slower a dog loses attention (keeps it longer). Of course within limits - if you take forever, your dog may walk away! ;-)

Similarly, when we move our arm *inwards* (*towards* our body), our dog will briefly concentrate on us. While when we move our arm *outwards* (*away* from our body), our dog should be concentrating on us considerably longer - even after our arm movement finished.

I believe this is because such outwards movement looks like an invitation gesture: "Hey look, I am opening my body up for you." - And the dog is thinking: "What's going to happen next?"

While when we move our arm inwards, we have to stop: Our body is in the way. And right there, our dog loses attention.

Play around a bit with speed and direction of your **Arm Movements**, and watch how your dog's attention is changing.

Second example: Hand Cues

Hand Cues are the more obvious way of using our body language as a Dog Training Tool.

Both Hand Cues and Arm Movements can also be used as Dog Commands (p~184). And indeed, giving our dog **visual cues rather than vocal commands** improves our dog-human relationship dramatically!

<u>Show - Don't Tell</u>

Calling Our Dog

When you call your dog, and (s)he isn't giving you **Attention** (coming to you, or at least looking at you), then this is a clear signal that your dog believes (s)he is the Pack leader, and thus <u>(s)he</u> decides when to come.

Conversely, when our dog *accepts* us as Pack leader, <u>or</u> when (s)he is experiencing a *conflict* in the Pack structure, in all such cases we can **Call Our Dog** to get the dog's **Attention**.

Note:

- The *less* we call our dog, the more likely that (s)he will come when finally called

- Instead of verbally <u>Calling Our Dog</u>, we can give a <u>Hand Cue</u> (if our dog can clearly see us)

- Try it out: Make sure your dog can see you, then give your chosen <u>Hand Cue</u> (use it consistently)

- Each form has its benefits depending on the situation (eg noise level, great distance, darkness), but training our dog to <u>Come On Hand Cue</u> improves the relationship (because **Dog Language is Body Language**) - and it will impress our neighbors ;-)

- Remember that whenever we **Call Our Dog** (vocally or visually), we <u>must</u> have something great - a great experience, a <u>Reward</u> (p~119) - or soon our dog won't come immediately anymore.

In addition to being an <u>Attention Tool</u> (p~170), <u>Calling Our Dog</u> also is a <u>Stimulant</u> (p~76), but there was no more space on the mindmap.

If calling your dog is a <u>Sedative</u> for your dog, you have a problem! ;-)

Standing Up

Standing Up is an <u>Attention Tool</u> (our dog will focus on *any* person who is standing up) as well as an <u>Energy Tool</u> - a <u>Stimulant</u> (p~76), it raises the dog's energy level.

Note the difference between **Standing Up** and <u>Calling Our Dog</u>: Normally, only the dog owner and (family) Pack members can raise the dog's attention by calling the dog, while *anyone* can raise our dog's attention by merely <u>Standing Up</u>.

Obviously the reason is that our dog doesn't know what's going to happen when someone's standing up, but the dog knows that it's better to be ready for **flight or fight**. That's why our dog will focus on *any* person who is <u>Standing Up</u>, *until* the dog is confident that neither flight nor fight is necessary.

Walking to the Dog

Walking to the dog will *raise* our dog's Attention because the dog is wondering *why* we are coming closer. It also is a Sedative (p~45).

Really, if your dog doesn't even blink an eye when you (or anyone else) are approaching, then something is wrong. Unless a dog is *clinically sedated*, a dog should always shift concentration towards *any* person approaching - whether Pack leader, Pack member, familiar person or stranger. Because dogs are energy recipients (p~39).

Once the dog knows what it's about (say, seeing us coming with the leash), attention fades. That's why it's double-wrong when dog owners walk to their dog and *show off* the Food Treat (p~134) they intend to give.

As with Standing Up (p~178), *anyone* can raise our dog's attention by walking to the dog. The dog will focus on any person who is approaching, *until* the dog is confident that neither flight nor fight is necessary:

- A dog that's <u>well socialized</u> will *not* storm towards that person for that infamous 'bark attack', but instead will remain calm on the spot, seemingly uninterested.

- A dog that's <u>well trained</u> will either come back to the dog owner, or will remain calm on the spot, seemingly uninterested.

- If the dog remains on the spot almost petrified, it's a clear sign that the dog is not confident (not mastering the situation like a relaxed dog would).

- If the dog hesitantly creeps *towards* that person and collects some patting, it's a clear sign that the dog is very trusting (maybe too much?).

Lip Licking

Lip Licking you found already under Energy Tools (Stimulants, p~79), so you know that when we make a gesture with or towards our mouth, our dog assumes that some food will be on the platter soon!

Lip Licking makes our dog wonder: "What's my Pack buddy/Pack leader savoring there, huh??"

Anything relating to food is a great Attention Tool, because it directly addresses the prime genetic quest of dogs: to secure food.

Sadly, this also is the reason for the majority of cases of mauled children:

- Children between the ages of 5 and 9 are 900 times(!) more likely to be bitten by a dog than even postmen/women!

- And almost half of all bites to children are on areas of the face!!

This is because children are not just thumb-sucking, but generally have their hands all too often at their mouth - signaling to any nearby dog: "What's that creature there savoring on, huh??"

So, if you have children in the house (or among relatives, friends), make sure that they learn to associate "Dog is present" with "Hands away from the mouth"!

Using Dog Commands

Obviously, whenever we give our dog a command, the dog should pay us attention. <u>Dog Commands</u> are an <u>Attention Tool</u> (p~170).

If in your case that's not the case, then this is a clear sign that your dog believes (s)he is the Pack leader!

The subsequent <u>Commands Little Helper</u> can help to record the commands you and your family want to use for your dog. Before you turn the page, brace yourself for some *very complex* form... ;-)

Command	Meaning
Example: Verbal cue: "SIT" Visual cue:	Buttocks on the ground, but front feet standing

Simple is best! - Not enough lines? No worries. a) You can extend the printed page yourself, and b) We won't excessively use commands anyway.

Remember, we **behavior-train** our dog, rather than command-train the dog (p~46).

Recording all **Dog Commands** as precise as possible is important, because without that our dog training would lack Consistency (p~75) - but Consistency is key for training success.

So, I would strongly encourage you to make use of that form (or make up your own) - even if you are the only one to interact with your dog (rarely the case). Because, we all are quick in *unknowingly* making small modifications to our Dog Commands. Our only savior is a precise dog commands description that's clinging to the fridge, say with some cute dog magnets so that we continue to *look* at them (my germanshepherd.org/go/paw-print-magnets).

What commands?

Generally, you can make up your own **Dog Command List**, and indeed in different geographies the Dog Commands *vary* more or less, even in the same language. However, Consistency is absolutely necessary, and if you are ever going to choose a professional dog trainer, you should use the same commands as (s)he does.

Conversely, if you aim to perform your own dog training and you realize how crucial Consistency is (p~75), then you may find the following **Dog Command Lists** useful.

Basic Dog Commands

Basic Dog Commands that apply to both situations, <u>On-leash</u> and <u>Off-leash</u>, are primarily the following:

- NO or STOP - to make your dog stop doing whatever (s)he is doing right now

- SIT - to make your dog sit at the current position

- DOWN to make your dog lie down at the current position

- STAND - to make your dog stand up when (s)he is in the SIT or DOWN position

- OFF - to make your dog get off the item (s)he is currently on

- STAY - to make your dog stay at the current position

- GO - to make your dog start walking or running

- FOCUS - to make your dog focus on you, and not be distracted

- SPEAK - to make your dog bark

- QUIET - to make your dog stop any whining or barking

- HEEL - to remind your dog to walk next to you, on either side, at your pace

- BITE - to make your dog bite into a given object

- OUT or DROP IT - to make your dog give free any item (s)he has in the mouth

- HOLD - to make your dog hold in the mouth whatever (s)he is biting on

Basic Dog Commands that apply to Off-Leash only:

- COME - to make your dog come towards you

- GO OUT - to make your dog leave the crate, kennel, room, or house

- GO IN - to make your dog enter the crate, kennel, room, or house

Advanced Dog Commands

If your dog training shall go any further than the above Basic Dog Commands, then you or your chosen dog trainer can teach your dog the more Advanced Dog Commands. Each such command may greatly enhance the joy both you and your dog will have in life:

- JUMP - to make your dog jump over any form of barrier

- BRING - to make your dog bring to you a shown item

- FETCH - to make your dog catch a shown item in the mouth

- LEAVE IT - to make your dog not pick up an item in the mouth

- BEHIND LEFT / BEHIND RIGHT - to make your dog walk around you on your left/right

- FIND - to make your dog search for a shown item or person

189

- TURN LEFT / TURN RIGHT - to make your dog change walking direction

- TRACK - to make your dog track and follow examples of a shown item

- GUARD - to make your dog watch over an object or person and stop it from moving

Note that all above commands are listed in the order of difficulty - as it concerns **Command Dog Training** *in general*. This means, your own dog may of course learn an individual Dog Command sooner or later than some other Dog Training Commands.

After all, this also depends on how, how intensely, and how consistently you or the professional dog trainer train your dog.

Both the Basic Dog Commands and the Advanced Dog Commands above are **Obedience Commands** or **Behavior Commands**. A different matter would be if you wish to teach your dog some tricks?

A bestseller book on trick training (including intuitive diagrams) is 101 Dog Tricks (mygermansh epherd.org/go/101-dog-tricks).

Most dogs learn best when we use a **Clicker** (mygermanshepherd.org/go/clicker). The reason is that **Clicker Training** standardizes the training (makes it *consistent*, yes!), so that dogs learn much faster and training success is more reliable (remembered for longer).

If you have come to appreciate the benefits of Clicker Training your dog: the top Clicker Training DIY course is Morten and Cecilie's Clicker Training: The 4 Secrets to Becoming a Supertrainer (which comprises both book and helpful videos).

Consistent Training Times

The importance of Consistency (p~75) in our Dog Training I mentioned already under Sedatives, and in Consistent Meal Times (p~162) under Food Tools.

Finally, **Consistent Training Times** are an Attention Tool because they allow the dog to build an *expectation* when we will be giving our dog a lot of attention again (which we do *most* during training). Thus our dog learns to be more attentive at those times.

Consistent Training Times alone can have a big impact on our Dog Training success. Because, unlike us, dogs don't get easily bored from routine behavior, they thrive on experiencing the same routine. This doesn't mean that dogs wouldn't love the surprise trip to the beach, the hiking trip, swimming in a river, a very tasty birthday morsel or whatever - they LOVE Real-Life Treats (p~127) and Food Treats (p~134). It just means that where humans easily *lose* attention upon routine behavior, canines don't. :-)

Make your Dog Training FUN and your dog will be even more attentive, because then (s)he learns to *expect* that the Together-time is FUN. Naturally, this will dramatically improve your bonding and relationship building!

Distraction Tools

On to the last Toolset - yeah!

Please note that **Distraction Tools** are the most demanding - not in terms of using them but in terms of understanding *some* of them. So please don't feel discouraged if at times this chapter may sound a bit 'too high' at first.

Let things 'sink in', **your Eureka moment** WILL come, just give it a bit time! It will all fall in place, like in a jigsaw, the more you'll be thinking about the Dog Training Tools, and the more you'll practice using them. Nothing can replace practice!

The moment you're thinking "OMG, what's he saying here?!", just leave this chapter alone and return later. Don't let this chapter ruin your joy and experience in using the other tools. Okay?

Distraction Tools are the opposite of Attention Tools (p~170). As the name suggests, Distraction Tools distract our dog from whatever (s)he is concentrating on. They *divert* our dog's attention (concentration, focus). Ideally they completely distract our dog.

- Most of the time, we want our dog to <u>disregard a stressful stimulus</u> - this is relatively easy (but not as easy as getting our dog's attention)

- Often we may need to turn our dog's attention *away from us*, namely deny excessive attention seeking (or we will outright seed future behavior problems!)

- Sometimes we may even want to help our dog to 'let go' (of a thought, of a memory of past experience). Say, in order to heal a traumatized dog (injured dog, shelter dog).

Note that some **Distraction Tools** are also <u>Energy Tools</u> (p~39), and again both Toolsets impact on our <u>dog's mindset</u> or mental state.

Instead of just repeating the differences between these two - which are similar to those I mentioned under <u>Attention Tools</u> (p~170) - here are some *new* differences:

- **Distraction** from a stressful stimulus can be achieved by *lowering* our dog's energy level (using Sedatives, p~45)

- However, **Distraction** can also be achieved by *raising* our dog's energy level (using Stimulants, p~76) - but this is dangerous if we cannot *control* our dog's energy level!

- A *low* energy level neither means we have a distracted dog nor that we have a concentrated dog - because **Distraction** too is energy-neutral

- **Distraction** is more difficult to achieve than Attention, but much quicker than to *lower* our dog's energy level.

Further differences between the two will become clearer as we progress.

Note that, in general, Attention Tools (p~170) can also (briefly) be used as Distraction Tools (while we are getting our dog to focus on us, instead of say on a stressful stimulus). However, the subsequent **Distraction Tools** are considerably better for the purpose of diverting our dog's attention - and particularly to 'let go' of the memory of past experience (ie for healing a traumatized dog, say from a shelter or prior owner).

Also note that in situations where we want to distract our dog from a <u>stressful stimulus</u>, we should either use Distraction Tools that are also <u>Sedatives</u> (p~45) or, for those that are not, we should *combine* them with Sedatives in order to *calm down* our dog.

Walking away

<u>Walking away</u> from our dog will (at least briefly) divert the dog's attention from whatever stimulus (s)he's concentrating on. This is regardless whether we are the accepted Pack leader or merely a Pack member (but we have to be either of the two, it does not work with strangers).

Canines' second-most important genetic quest is to belong to a <u>Pack</u> (the most important is to secure food). This <u>focus on its Pack</u> dominates any stimulus the dog is experiencing *outside* the Pack (except food). Exception, as always: Traumatized dogs.

When we walk *away* from our dog, we signal: "I don't care about that stimulus that seems to bother you". So the dog is thinking: "Hm, should I care then?"

However, whether our dog now *follows* us (disregards the stimulus), depends on the individual situation, eg:

- extent of perceived 'danger'

- how fast we go away

- our dog's past experience with us going away

- whether we are *accepted* Pack leader, etc.

But the key is: **Walking away** from our dog <u>does distract</u> the dog!

Turning Away

We don't necessarily need to <u>walk away</u> from our dog (p~197) - and if (s)he is on the leash this would be difficult anyway without *pulling* the dog (which we better always avoid).

In many situations we can simply **Turn Around** to face the other direction.

Say, there's an aggressive dog walking past on the other side of the road, and we don't want our dog to react in any way (we don't want to increase the other dog's aggression, ha!). So, we <u>Turn Around</u>!

But note that this <u>Distraction Tool</u> (p~193) requires that we are our dog's *accepted* Pack leader - how to achieve this you saw already with prior tools of our DOG TRAINING TOOLKIT, namely the <u>Feeding Routine</u> (p~138).

If we are not the *accepted* Pack leader, but our dog believes (s)he is the Pack leader, then (s)he will continue to focus on whatever stimulus there is - believing (s)he has to protect us. And in case of an aggressive dog walking past, our dog will probably storm towards that dog, unless (s)he is on the <u>Short Leash</u> (p~83) or scared of that dog.

In some situations, **Turning Sideways** is smarter, because then we can still see what our dog (or anyone's dog) is doing.

with Stick

...divert our dog's attention towards a stick or anything else we find on the ground.

Our task is to make a theater performance (yes, again!): We pretend this random object is so exceptionally interesting that our dog gets curious to see what we have there. We probably bend down to look at the 'stick', partially hide it in our hand, and overall seem absolutely *astonished* what we just found at this inconspicuous location. :-)

Whether facilitating a twig, stick, leaf or whatever - a good performance is as much FUN as it distracts our dog (as you can see in his videos Doggy Daniel uses this a lot, alone or together with other Tools: mygermanshepherd.org/go/online-dog-trainer).

Sitting Down

A simple manoeuvre like <u>Sitting Down</u> is able to *briefly* distract a dog in many situations.

Why only briefly? Obviously because, once we sit we need something else!

Gladly, this <u>Distraction Tool</u> (p~193) *does* come with something else: It also is a <u>Sedative</u> (p~45), and if its *calming effect* continues where the distraction ends, this tool alone can very well be enough to make our dog 'let go' of say a stressful stimulus.

Ignoring Attention Seeking

Although ignoring excessive Attention Seeking certainly is a Dog Training Tool (a powerful one!), it feels a bit clumsy to add it here to Distraction Tools.

Nonetheless it fits here best because, when we *ignore* our dog in a certain situation, we divert the dog's attention *away from us* to attend to something else instead. So yes, we **distract** our dog.

Note that in some cases Ignoring Attention Seeking is not a standalone Dog Training Tool but may require that we use additional Tools. Namely when our dog continually nudges us or even nips us, we may need to use a hand cue or other body language (p~172), or stand up (p~179) or walk away (p~197).

Ignoring Attention Seeking means we do not reward excessive Attention Seeking with ... *Attention*! No Praise (p~119), no Affection (p~120), no Toys or Play (p~124), no Food Treats (p~134), and no looking, speaking, or touching at this moment.

If our dog already has a Toy at its disposal (say in the crate or on a Resting Place, p~65), fine. But we will not at this moment provide a Toy. Because if we do or give any of the above, we would effectively *train* our dog to come to us and seek our attention every few minutes. This is not a 'loving dog' (what many dog owners desire to believe), this is a very *stressed* dog - and stress is bad for dogs!

Therefore, when we feel that our dog excessively seeks our attention (think of puppies!), it is crucial that for the next few minutes our dog *finds* something to get occupied with. We must not interfere, we do not provide anything now.

Some earlier readers misunderstood this advice (Ignoring Attention Seeking). They got the impression that we must not give attention to our dog *anytime* the dog is coming to us "because the dog loves us".

No, that's not what I mean. When our dog is seeking our attention, we *should* first give this our attention - we should be thinking:

- Hmm, is it time for a meal (p~161) already?

- For a walk (p~164)?

- Filling up the drinking bowl (p~54)?

- Is our dog in pain?

- Alarming us of 'danger'?

- Wants to play (p~100) because it's our usual playtime?

- Wants a Food Treat (p~169) because '(s)he normally gets one'?

- What's the reason??

So, we certainly give our dog attention! Our dog's Attention Seeking should make us THINK.

But do we REACT? This should depend on the outcome of the above considerations, because some dogs almost *permanently* seek their owner's attention, and that is <u>not</u> a sign of love but of <u>dependency</u>!

If you now give in, you would nurture this dependency, and thus outright *seed* future 'dog problems': In a dog pack this does never happen. Already as a puppy, if mum or litter mates find "it's too much!", they ignore the pup completely.

If you give your dog the impression (s)he is "the most important living being" - even if (s)he is for you - then you make your dog suffer <u>Separation</u>

Anxiety (mygermanshepherd.org/periodical/germ an-shepherd-dog-separation-anxiety-cure - watch it, relevant regardless of breed), even at times when you are at home! Your dog would be *permanently* stressed (on a high energy level). This stress <u>will</u> lead to health and behaviour problems. Thus if you love your dog (see the book title), then by all means *don't* give in to excessive Attention Seeking!

To be relaxed, a dog <u>must</u> be allowed to 'switch off' completely for several hours each day. 'Switching off' means, our dog does not seek our attention whatsoever. Mental freedom of *both* of the two most fundamental canine quests: Securing food, and belonging to a Pack. Okay?

If you notice that your dog is seeking your attention almost permanently during awake hours, then don't even for a second think "I would be cruel if I turn my dog away". No, the opposite is true: If you allow your dog to be dependent on you <u>in terms of time</u>, *then* you would be cruel because your dog will suffer.

The only dependencies of domesticated dogs on us humans which lead to health and behavior problems when *withheld* are:

1. that we provide sufficient water regularly

2. that we provide sufficient food regularly

3. that we socialize to provide a Pack feeling

4. and that we provide sufficient potty walks.

Because the first three are the dependencies that have been bred into our domesticated dogs for at least 50,000 dog generations (see again the chapter All Pack members close by, p~69). And the last has only become a dependency because we keep our domesticated dogs inside the house with front door closed. Thus our dogs cannot go for a pee every 20 minutes or so (like wild dogs do because the canine bladder is prone to infections if not emptied frequently).

While providing shelter, Affection (p~120), Toys & Play (p~124), tasty Food Treats (p~134) or even a fashion coat (mygermanshepherd.org/go/fashion-coat) are recent developments too new to bear genetic significance: We do all of this for no more than maybe 150 years, and a few hundred dog generations are not enough to genetically manifest dependencies that would lead to behavior or health problems when *withheld*.

So don't you worry about 'withholding love' when you ignore excessive Attention Seeking - if you've come as far as to this page I am sure you're giving your dog enough love. ;-)

How to Ignore the Right Way

If our dog permanently nudges the nose into our lap, it's not easy to ignore such excessive Attention Seeking without doing something about it. So what's the right way to ignore our dog in such moment?

- First, give the <u>potential reasons for Attention Seeking</u> some consideration (p~204)

- If none meets your case, you can <u>Walk away</u> (p~197) or <u>Turn away</u> (p~199)

- Do not use force whatsoever!

- Don't speak, don't look, don't touch

- If you can't avoid it, use the <u>outside of your arm</u> to *gently* turn away your dog (or anyone's dog)

- Where not possible, use the <u>back of your hand</u> in a *slow movement* (you don't want to raise aggression, you merely want to signal "not now darling")

- For successful **Distraction** <u>minimal touch</u> is crucial here

- If despite the above your dog (or anyone's dog) continues to seek your attention <u>two more times</u>, then upon the third time I would <u>get up</u> and *gently* do the <u>Collar Freeze</u> (p~51)

- If you want, and you have a <u>Short Leash</u> (p~83) at hand, you can alternatively do some <u>SSCD</u> (p~61).

Whatever of these measures you have to take, this will successfully **distract** your dog from seeking your attention (and being stressed) - <u>without</u> the need for any force, or raising fear, or giving morsels, or using 'gadgets collars', or pulling or pushing, or shouting. This simple and *gentle* Behavior Training is most effective to build the best relationship with your dog.

The typical outcome is that the dog will calmly lie down. In any case, it allows the dog to 'switch off' completely - from *both* of the most fundamental canine quests. This relaxation is crucial for the well-being of our domesticated dogs.

Toys and Play

In addition to being <u>Stimulants</u> (p~76), Toys and Play also are great <u>Distraction Tools</u> (p~193).

<u>Play</u> *more* than most <u>Toys</u>, because during Play (as we define it here) <u>we interact</u> with our dog, while with many Toys we typically let our dog play on its own (nonetheless, for safety reasons we *must* casually observe the dog, I mentioned that).

However, all the Toys that require that we interact with our dog - see <u>Activity Toys</u> (p~95), <u>Puzzle Toys</u> (p~97) and <u>Tug Toys</u> (p~98) - are excellent **Distraction Tools**.

Toys that significantly challenge a dog's physical *and* mental skills are best for this: Puzzle Toys. This is why sophisticated Puzzle Toys like Nina Ottoson's wooden puzzle treat toys (mygermanshepherd.org/go/wooden-dog-puzzle-toys) are so immensely helpful to heal traumatized dogs.

SSCD

In addition to being a <u>Sedative</u> (p~45), <u>SSCD</u> (p~61) also is a great <u>Distraction Tool</u> (p~193) whenever we have a <u>Short Leash</u> (p~83) at hand.

The added beauty: This is true regardless whether our dog hates the leash or not. If the dog hates the leash (wrong introduction to Leash Training! - see mygermanshepherd.org/go/leash-training-guide) then SSCD will take longer to *calm down* our dog, but the <u>Distraction</u> through SSCD is immediate none-theless.

This is why **SSCD** is such a great Dog Training Tool to distract from a stressful stimulus - *even if* a dog hates the leash. Obviously, in cases where the leash itself is the stressful stimulus, we will <u>not</u> use SSCD. That would be punishment (wannabe intellectuals call it "negative reinforcement") - which really is a *bad* training method for dogs (see <u>Partner</u>, p~115). Instead, we will then use other <u>Distraction Tools</u>, including (the in this case urgent) <u>Desensitization</u> (p~217) from the <u>Short Leash</u> (p~83)!

Isolation

Isolation we use for <u>serious misconduct</u> (any form of biting or uninvited nipping - this would be considered serious by mum and litter mates too!), or for <u>persistent lighter misconduct</u> (say, chewing our shoes repetitively). Compare this with the <u>Collar Freeze</u> (p~51).

Uninvited nipping: any nipping outside <u>controlled Play-fighting</u> (p~104).

What is Isolation?

Upon <u>serious misconduct</u> or <u>persistent lighter misconduct</u>, we immediately but calmly <u>walk to</u> our dog, *gently* take hold of the collar on the *underside* (not at the neck!), and lead the dog into **Isolation**: a small safe room, like for example a small tiled bathroom or any other room with as few distractions and furniture as possible.

A small tiled bathroom/toilet room with an <u>indoor potty</u> (mygermanshepherd.org/go/ugodog) is ideal for this, *even if* our dog is not yet housebroken (see

House Training Dogs to Behave Well in a High Value Home: mygermanshepherd.org/go/house-training-gu ide).

Although there is no reason to be upset if the dog is going to urinate while in **Isolation** (we just clean it up), with an <u>indoor potty</u> in the safe room, there is a chance that our dog may urinate on the indoor potty, rather than on the tiles (and once potty trained, a good chance indeed).

We isolate our <u>adult dog</u> for a minimum of 15 minutes and otherwise until totally calm (no barking, whining, or scratching at the door). Just note the following points for **Isolation** to be both <u>effective and safe</u>:

- When we *calmly* lead our dog into the safe room, we don't speak, we don't touch, and we don't look at our dog (the more apathetic, the better)

- We only let our dog out of Isolation when (s)he is totally calm, not as long as the dog is barking, whining, or scratching at the door (<u>door scratch-guards</u> can help here: mygermanshepherd.org/ go/door-scratchguard)

- If not calm after 20 to 30 min, we take a <u>bowl of water</u> inside, put it down and leave (again, no speaking, no touching, no looking) - may sound crazy but it really is the best reaction!

- If needed, every 20 to 30 min we pretend to only want to fill up the water

- Just in case your dog is still not calm after <u>two hours</u> (max! - very unlikely), I would suggest to end the **Isolation** nonetheless

- When we end the Isolation, <u>we simply open the door to the safe room</u> (again, no speaking, no touching, no looking), and we go back to do whatever we were doing (or if time for a <u>walk</u> we do just that, p~64)

- So: We must continue to <u>ignore</u> our dog for a while, after our dog got out of <u>Isolation</u>. This is crucial! It helps our dog to understand that (s)he did something wrong

- Only when we have finished what we were doing (or after say a further 30 min max), <u>we call our dog to us</u>, and *then* we act as if all is good, ie we give our dog a great experience (see Reward Tools, p~119).

Play (Together-time, p~125) would be ideal now, because it helps our dog to realize what a big difference there is between being **isolated** and being close to its Pack (p~69).

Why no speaking, no touching, no looking?

Because all dogs understand our body language (p~172) and tone of voice (p~119) much better than the words that come from our mouth - and we must avoid that we communicate our feelings *in any way* in such moment of distress! That's why I said "the more apathetic, the better".

Why waiting until totally calm?

Because this is the *earliest* moment when it starts to sink in: When our dog may realize that its behavior is not what we want.

As long as our dog is not totally calm, (s)he obviously is on a higher energy level (during Isolation initially often higher than 5, watch Doggy Dan: mygermanshepherd.org/go/online-dog-train er). While on a higher energy level, even the smartest dogs cannot think, reflect, and understand well, because of their stressed mental state.

This is why <u>trained protection dogs</u> are particularly *calm* dogs, otherwise they couldn't assess new situations well (which is the key skill of a protection dog). When you see a teeth-fledging, growling dog in front of a property, you are seeing an *aggressive* dog, not a trained protection dog.

Why ignoring for a bit longer?

Because only at this point (when *out* of Isolation but not yet reunited with its Pack) our dog will understand that its *earlier* behavior (the serious misconduct or persistent lighter misconduct) was not what we wanted. By giving <u>Attention</u> (p~170) <u>on our terms</u> we help our dog to make that connection.

This is what prevents repetition of the misconduct - either immediately or soon after the dog experienced two or three <u>Isolations</u> for the same misconduct (exactly like with the <u>Collar Freeze</u>, p~51).

Why is Isolation so Effective?

Isolation is so effective because it directly addresses the second-most fundamental canine quest: The inherent canine desire to belong to a Pack - at least as Pack member (but ideally as accepted Pack leader).

An isolated dog instinctively realizes that (s)he is excluded from a Pack, from *any* Pack! No dog likes this, because it goes against the canine genetical heritage. In fact, I don't know of any breed where the breeders have successfully eliminated this canine quest! All domesticated dogs (unless traumatized) desire to be close to human Pack members (see p~112).

Maybe you are now wondering: "If Isolation directly addresses the second-most fundamental canine quest, isn't it then a means 'too cruel' to be applied to our dog - even if (s)he has bitten me?"

This is human thinking but, as much as we know, not how dogs think. For dogs (and for puppies too), the short **Isolation** is just the right amount of feedback - which they get in their dog pack too: When you watch **Litter Socialization** of puppies, you can observe exactly the same. For more, see the Puppy Development Guide - Puppy 101 (mygerma nshepherd.org/go/puppy-development-guide).

However, note that Isolation is <u>reactive dog training</u>. So, if we have to isolate our dog due to *biting*, we should better have done some Bite Inhibition training (p~72) - which is <u>proactive dog training</u>. Obviously it's always easier to prevent 'dog problems' rather than having to cure them.

Desensitization

Desensitization means that we make our dog less sensitive towards a specific stressful stimulus (eg the vacuum cleaner, the <u>Short Leash</u> (p~83), motor-bikers, playing children, our cat, other dogs, rabbits and squirrels, etc). So that in future we no longer need to use a <u>Distraction Tool</u> (p~193) in such situations.

Desensitization is more an <u>overall training approach</u> than an individual Dog Training Tool, because it actually requires us to use any number and combination of Dog Training Tools already discussed above (which is why I bring it at the *end* of the Dog Training Toolkit).

As there are unlimited situations where you may want to **desensitize** your dog from a stressful stimulus, it is impossible to make everyone happy with the description of this Tool. Also remember that the purpose of this book is to *introduce* you to the Dog Training Toolkit, for its *application* to numerous more dog training situations see later the Adult Dog Behavior <u>Training Compendium</u> (mygermanshepherd.org/go/training-compendium).

Nonetheless, again here is an <u>example</u> how to apply this Tool.

Desensitization Example

Say our dog goes berserk when we use the vacuum cleaner (entirely normal, most dogs do). The penetrating noise is too much to bear! For dogs and for myself (I go berserk too, ha!).

Obviously we don't want to stop cleaning the house - particularly not if our dog's shedding is the prime reason for much of the cleaning (mygermanshep herd.org/periodical/german-shepherd-shedding).
But we don't want to torture our dog either, right?

So what can we do?

1. We divide the entire process that leads up to the stressful stimulus into individual phases

2. We introduce our dog to each individual phase, and allow the dog to get used to it - while we <u>distract</u> the dog (p~193)

3. We then introduce our dog to small combined individual phases - before we expose the dog again to the entire process.

In terms of the vacuum cleaning it could look like this:

1. We <u>Play</u> a bit with our dog (p~100)

2. We get out the vacuum cleaner, towards the other end of the room

3. We continue playing a bit with our dog

4. We turn on the feisty machine (obviously lowest setting)

5. We play a bit longer with our dog (while demonstratively not giving the machine any attention!)

6. We go over and merely pick up the suction hose, then put it back down

7. We play a bit with our dog (demonstratively making nothing of the machine)

8. We go over and make one or two cleaning movements

9. We play a bit with our dog (demonstratively ignoring the machine)

10. And we slowly increase the cleaning period and play periods!

Play (with or without a Toy, p~124) is a great **Distraction Tool** for Desensitization, because the interaction with our dog distracts way better than say just giving our dog a Chew Toy (p~94) to play with, *hoping* this would be able to distract the dog (what apparently most dog owners then try).

Obviously you can use any combination of Sedatives (p~45) and Distraction Tools (p~193), and you can split the process as you see fit in your particular situation.

Actually, in Dan's online video dog training library there is even a video of a client appointment where he performs **vacuum cleaning desensitization** (my germanshepherd.org/go/online-dog-trainer)!

The general process for Desensitization always is step 1, 2, and 3 above (p~221).

The End

This concludes the DOG TRAINING TOOLKIT presented in this book, which gives us a good structure of tons of Dog Training Tools we can refer to when faced with any 'dog problem'.

What Next?

As pointed out earlier, 'dog problems' are often _normal_ behavior of an animal that we humans perceive as a problem.

Therefore, in some cases it may be sensible to just accept our dog's behavior (ignore it), while in other cases it may seem necessary to modify our dog's behavior. Both cases we can now address, because we have plenty of Dog Training Tools to go with.

We even have a <u>Mindmap</u> (p~34) to help us memorize the Tools and to remember which Tool is suitable in what situation, and why! But note: Ultimately, nothing can replace **practice**. _Knowing_ that the Tools exist and what they do is not enough, we must **use the Tools**.

Many dog owners send desperate requests for help to our site, like for example:

- "My 11 month old mail dog wants to always jump on me and counter....help!!" - [she meant _male_ dog]

- "If I try to pull her away she growls and barks and pulls. If I let her approach, she runs and jumps on the other dog. Help!"

- "I have a four month old female dog. She is very mouthy and I am having a hard time getting her to stop biting. She also chases my cats, and nothing I do seems to work. I tried your collar freeze but she just grabs whatever part of my had or arm she can reach while I reach under her neck for her collar. HELP!!!" - [don't know what she meant with "my *had* or arm"]

- "Over the past 6 months he has become excessively aggressive to nearly everyone except us and our close family. Barking like a wild thing and scaring people to death with his lunging. He has always been the pack leader and now he will only come to heel for my husband. My husband mentioned having him out down….. What can I do?? I love my dogs more than anything, but if someone gets bitten…… Help!!"

- "The reason I'm writing anything is because she nipped my nephew on his leg while she was on a leash but he walked too close? Too fast? I don't know...he is fine more shaken up than anything but I don't know what to do with her. Help! My husband is so upset he wants to put her down and she's my baby!"

It always turns out that they haven't strictly applied what (mostly) they *know* they should <u>do</u>. In such case of course I can't help either. I can't *force* dog owners to study our Periodicals or my books. That would mean 'Obedience Training' them, ha! ;-)

If *you* have a problem with your dog, please first **use the Tools** from the Dog Training Toolkit, and only if your problem then persists (unlikely!) then please get in touch on our site, and I will personally look after you and your dog. :-)

In any case, there is no need to give your dog to a shelter (or do worse), every 'dog problem' can be solved. Obviously, the *sooner* you act, the better. Ideally *prevent* problems (<u>proactive dog training</u>, p~43, p~219).

Remember, **Behavior Training** means that primarily **we use our own behavior** to <u>motivate</u> our dog to do what we want. This *always* replaces all forms of <u>punishment</u> (force, fear, yelling, pushing and pulling, 'training collars' etc) and treat training. In many cases it replaces the use of <u>Commands</u> too (p~184).

In any case, **Behavior Training** improves the dog-human relationship dramatically! Apply it, and you too will enjoy it. - Plus, you will have more FUN along the way. **Behavior Training is FUN**. - While Obedience Training gives nightmares (certainly the dog).

The DOG TRAINING TOOLKIT clearly has the potential to change the world

For *all* dog owners and dogs alike!

The DOG TRAINING TOOLKIT should enable you to tackle <u>every</u> adult dog training situation that might occur in your family. Because you now have an abundance of **Tools** of which you know <u>why they work</u>, <u>how they work</u>, and <u>when they work</u> (ie you know their *structure*).

But, *because* of the abundance of Tools, I anticipate that some dog owners (who are not professional dog trainers) might now struggle to "see the wood for the trees", right?

Maybe you are wondering: "Wow! He showed me more options than I ever imagined to exist! - But what do I now actually DO in a challenging situation? The sheer number of Tools leave me confused."

If this case is your case, then please remember the important note I made already on p~32:

If, despite *applying* the advice you just read (practice), after a few weeks you still feel overwhelmed by the amount of new content here, then take one step back and <u>start easy</u>:

Both you and your dog will already be MUCH happier once you <u>simply replace all force and fear</u> with Collar Freeze (p~51) and Isolation (p~211)

(now linked :-)

Also remember: While the <u>canine traits</u> are the same for *all* canines, <u>learned behaviors</u> (learned through training or traumatization!) can of course be very different with individual dogs:

1) Your <u>dog's past experience</u> (in your family pack and before) and thus the dog's memories

2) and your <u>dog's present living environment</u> and situation (health, housing, feeding, exercise, etc)

3) and your way of <u>interacting with your dog</u> (eg *how* you apply a particular Dog Training Tool, how you behave, etc)

...all of these *change* over time and are *different* to another person's dog. This is why no dog training tool can ever yield the same results for everyone in every situation (and this is why I believe that the *structure* I gave the Tools is so helpful).

The above should be obvious but I need to mention it anyway to avoid complaints (that you always get from *someone*, regardless how helpful you are). Thus, what doesn't work well with your dog today, may work well tomorrow. Or it may work well for *your* dog but not as well for your neighbor's dog (whether today or tomorrow). Okay?

That's why I always encourage every dog owner, and now you too:

1. Look at the Dog Training Toolkit (mindmap)

2. Pick a Tool that seems sensible in your present situation, and

3. **Try it out, use it!**

If it requires continued application, apply it consistently (p~75). If needed, apply another Tool, in addition or instead. **Practice makes perfect**, once you know your Tools and how to use them. Like it is for the auto-mechanic, the builder, the plumber, the cook, and anyone else who needs to use Tools.

If you have any idea what I can improve in this **Dog Training Toolkit**, let me know: support@my germanshepherd.org - Thanks!

If instead or in addition you'd like to post a review for this book, then I will definitely see and read your review here:

- amazon.com/review/create-review/?asin=
  B00DVXVE2Q

- amazon.co.uk/review/create-review/?asin=
  B00DVXVE2Q

- amazon.ca/review/create-review/?asin=
  B00DVXVE2Q

More Books by the Same Author

House Training Dogs to Behave Well in a High Value Home (mygermanshepherd.org/go/house-training-guide)

House Training is much more than housebreaking; it is *everything* to get your dog to behave well in the house while having free run of the house while you are away!

- "I found this book hugely informative. There is so much stuff in here that I didnt know, and it has already helped me with my four month old puppy. Housetraining and housebreaking are truly very different things"

- "I was amazed how much I thought I knew but really failed in my conception of family life with a GSD. The information was spot on. The book after reading it twice is a real eye opener and a must for dog owners"

- "Wonderful book/guide, very simple to use methods, the results are phenomenal"

- "Excellent Guide!! Lots of great ideas and not too technical. Tim writes with the DOG in mind with emphasis on not over-thinking, over-correcting or over-training. I have used many of his methods and suggestions successfully"

Puppy Development Guide - Puppy 101: The Secrets to Puppy Training Without Force, Fear, and Fuss (mygermanshepherd.org/go/puppy-development-guide)

- "Best Training Book I have ever read"
- "Puppy must-have!"
- "Easy to read even experienced dog owners can get something from this book"

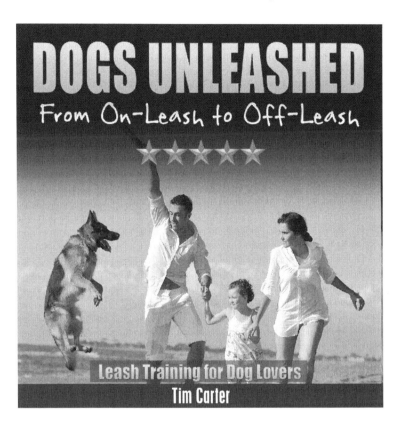

Dogs Unleashed - From On-Leash to Off-Leash
(mygermanshepherd.org/go/leash-training-guide)

For when your dog pulls, lunges, won't heel, runs off, or doesn't come back when you call.

Even explains the equipment you need - and which you don't need!

amzn.to/19aD72r

amzn.to/1cNyokY

amzn.to/1c2R676

amzn.to/JkSprf

Not to forget!

1. Please make sure your dog is <u>spayed/neutered</u>!

- It is still possible to alter an adult dog, yes.

- Just note that if you spay/neuter an **adult dog**, it may *temporarily* show some unpleasant behavioral changes, particularly in the first 3 to 12 months after the surgical intervention an increase in aggression (both towards animals and towards humans/you)

- However, this can be successfully controlled if you choose the right dog training approach, like the one we recommend and feature here, which is based on your <u>acceptance</u> as Pack leader

- More about spaying/neutering here: mygerman shepherd.org/periodical/gsd-spaying-and-neu tering

2. Please <u>do visit the vet regularly</u>. Once a year is the absolute minimum, because one year for us is between 6 and 12 years(!) for our dog (mygermansh epherd.org/german-shepherd-age-how-old-does-my-dog-think-it-is), depending on breed. The best and

cheapest outcome for us is then that each time the vet concludes: "Your dog is fine!"

3. However, please <u>do not simply nod through</u> every treatment a vet suggests. Our aim should always be to <u>get the correct diagnosis,</u> and to <u>then use the most</u> <u>*appropriate* treatment with the *least* long-term side effects</u>.

- A great example: The top ear infection remedy *Zymox Otic* is available *with* hydrocortisone and *without* hydrocortisone.

- Hydrocortisone is a corticosteroid, a hormone, and as such it can have dramatic side effects with impact on seemingly unrelated body functions!

- Hence our priority should be to <u>use Zymox Otic</u> <u>*without* hydrocortisone</u> (mygermanshepherd.org/ go/ear-treatment-without-cortisone).

4. Since we are at it, <u>before</u> you use any ear solution, you must <u>get your dog's eardrums checked by a vet</u>: If a solution is instilled into an ear canal with a perforated eardrum, it will enter the middle ear and

damage structures essential to hearing! Then the solution is no 'solution' but a problem.

5. Always <u>aim for antibiotic-free remedies</u>.

- Do NOT get caught up in the myth that antibiotics are 'a generally suitable blanket treatment for infections'.

- No, antibiotics are a generally *unsuitable* and typically *unnecessary* treatment - and *always* lead to chronic side effects that will sooner or later become apparent!

- Eg orally administered antibiotics impair the gastrointestinal wall, resulting in chronic excess gas and life-long intoxication of the blood stream (thus often shortened life)!

- Mark that: They are *anti*biotics - which means <u>against life</u>.

- For almost every condition there exist <u>more effective</u> <u>natural</u> remedies that have less side effects.

- The *only* exception when to use antibiotics: a *life-threatening* condition of our dog.

Much more information on all the above points you can of course soon find in the Health Compendium.

6. Consider micro-chipping your dog (mygermansh epherd.org/periodical/micro-chipping-your-dog). Particularly dogs of certain breeds are prone to get stolen with the purpose to sell them, or dognapped for various reasons. In any case (ie regardless where you live), dogs do commonly get lost often indeed!

7. Please do consider to get a dog from a rescue center/ shelter. - "Do not breed or buy while shelter dogs die!"

Did I forget other important points?
Is there anything how I could improve this book?
Feedback much appreciated:
mailto: support@mygermanshepherd.org -
Will add to next edition!

Most importantly, a final note:

A Dog's Life is Fairly Short

so Make Sure You

ENJOY Your Dog! :-)

Every day is a new chance to put things right.

Made in the USA
San Bernardino, CA
08 September 2017